wild australia

Photographs Theo Allofs
Text Nicola Markus

David Bateman

Copyright © photographs Theo Allofs, 2006
Copyright © text Nicola Markus, 2006
Copyright © David Bateman Ltd, 2006

Published 2006 by David Bateman Ltd,
30 Tarndale Grove, Albany, Auckland, New Zealand

Distributed in Australia by Brumby Books,
10 Southfork Driver, Kilsyth, Victoria

ISBN-10: 1-86953-613-4
ISBN-13: 978-1-86953-613-8

This book is copyright. Except for the purpose of fair review, no part may be stored or transmitted in any form or by any means, electronic or mechanical, including recording or storage in any information retrieval systems, without permission in writing from the publisher. No reproduction may be made, whether by photocopying or by any other means, unless a licence has been obtained from the publisher or its agent.

Design Think Red, Auckland
Printed in China by Everbest Printing Co.

Contents

Acknowledgements	5
Introduction: great southern land	6
Beyond the Horizon: Western Australia	28
Kakadu & Crocodiles: the 'top end'	60
Blue Sky, Red Earth: red centre	88
Tropical Treasures: Queensland's north	126
Koala Country: eucalypt forests of the south-east	154
Related Reading	190
Index	191

acknowledgements

The worries about not getting the images I needed for this book were largely reduced by the many friendly and supportive people I met during nine trips 'down under', where I spent almost two years waiting for the right moments in nature.

Thank you to Dr. Karen Coombes and her husband Neil, Margit Cianelli, and Bob Buckley and Beth Stirn, for their hospitality and help with my photography on the Atherton Tableland. Pam and Greg Taylor of Fur n' Feathers made it possible for me to find a wild cassowary with chicks. Dr. Les Hall, Dr. Hugh Spencer, Jenny Mclean and the late Chris Holman helped me to a great extent with my flying fox story. Thank you to Michael and Kim Moore for assisting me with my snake photography. Tourism Holdings Ltd Australia supplied excellent vehicles that enabled me to cross the vast outback deserts and gave comfortable shelter during tropical downpours. I am especially indebted to Michelle Chubb and Joe Sambono for their hospitality and great support with my flying fox and snake images. And what would I have done without the devotion of their son Joseph Sambono and his partner Corinne Hanlon. Many images in this book are the result of their support and great knowledge about reptiles.

Big hugs for my sister-in-law Heidi and her husband, Don Dixon, for giving me a home away from home between my months long walkabouts. Their cheerfulness and Heidi's delicious dinners helped me to forget the lonely and often frustrating weeks waiting for the right light.

And, dear Nicki, thank you for so many things: for being a good friend, for answering innumerable questions, for supplying me with the right contacts in Australia, for the great dinners together and especially for the excellent text accompanying my pictures in this book.

A book project isn't worth anything without a good publisher. Many thanks to Paul Bateman, for his interest in this topic, to associate publisher Tracey Borgfeldt for her invaluable advice, reliability and pleasant cooperation and to Richard Wheatley for the excellent layout.

Last but not least, I would like to thank my wife Sabine for her love, patience and moral support which gave me the strength to be away from home for months at a time...no worries, mates, with all your help the book is finally done.

Theo Allofs, 2006

Researching the many faces of Australia's landscapes was an amazing, and in some ways profound, journey of discovery that opened new horizons. The more I became immersed in the subject matter, the more I wanted to expand on my own small area of expertise. Thank you Theo for offering me this fantastic opportunity. I'm eternally grateful for that marvellous invention, the internet, for providing ready access to reliable websites that supplemented the facts I gathered from books, journeys and many conversations, alongside juggling my 'other' job.

However, my particular thanks go to a number of knowledgeable people who reviewed individual sections of this book and whose expertise and critique helped to sharpen the text. I'm grateful to David Croft, Peggy Eby, David Edey, Jarrad Holmes, Julie Kirkwood, Rick Leck, Colleen O'Malley, Bill McDonald, Richard McLellan, Ray Nias, Paul Sattler, Tanya Vernes and Mary E. White who provided insightful and constructive comments on sections of earlier drafts of this manuscript. Tracey Borgfeldt, Caroline McFarlane and Michael Mikhov road-tested the overall text, and Christel Markus provided ongoing inspiration and research assistance. Of course, the final text is my own and I take sole responsibility for its accuracy and any errors of interpretation of facts that may have crept in.

Nicola Markus, 2006

A small river on the Kimberley coast meanders over mud flats in the remote northernmost region of Western Australia.

Introduction
great southern land

There are many ways to experience a natural landscape for the first time. Most fundamentally, there are the physical features that give it contours and shape and the flora and fauna that bring it to life. With a more artistic eye, a landscape can be appreciated through a richer perception of detail — the melding of colours and textures, a sense of motion conveyed by wind, water, clouds or a flying bird, and an awareness of the scents and sounds that permeate the scenery.

The nature of the experience is in the eye of the beholder, however, and so any 'pure' impressions are invariably tempered by the culture, education, past experience or expectations of the eye's owner.

Conservation biologists have a very specific view of landscapes that rarely reflects the perceptions of the broader community. Their comparatively greater insight into certain aspects of nature imbues them with something of an x-ray perspective of the environment that sees the assemblage of features — soil, water courses, vegetation cover, wildlife and geology — and bores deeper for evidence of processes such as climate change, rainfall patterns, fragmentation, land use and other influences. The consideration of natural history and evolution may also come into play, and pretty soon the first impression of a newly encountered landscape in a land like Australia becomes a quick assessment of the degree of 'naturalness' remaining. The upside of this is a deep appreciation and empathy for the landscapes and the many challenges they weather; the downside is a profound awareness of the fragility of this ancient continent and its susceptibility to lasting damage if we don't respect its limitations.

Perhaps it is simply a reflection of human nature that the remarkable natural features of Australia — the unique wildlife, arid-adapted plants and time-honed mountain ranges and plains that make up this continent — are often under-appreciated in favour of the constructs of our urban surroundings. This is partly explained by the comparatively recent arrival in Australia, only 220 years ago, of the willing and unwilling settlers who sought to recreate the homes they had left behind on these very different shores. Unlike Australia's indigenous Aboriginal peoples who had lived as an integral part of and with the country for millennia, the new arrivals came as foreigners with no sense of the land. Shaped by a multi-cultural heritage comprising firstly English, Irish, German and Chinese, and later Greek, Italian, Japanese, and other Asian and Middle-Eastern traditions, modern Australian culture has been deeply infused with foreign ideals that focus on what the landscape may yield for human needs

Walls of China at sunrise after a rain storm, Mungo National Park, New South Wales. The Walls of China consists of alternate layers of sand and clay that were formed from a dry lake bed. The site has undergone severe erosion as introduced sheep and rabbits have overgrazed the vegetation that held these dunes in place. Mungo National Park is a site of great significance to Aboriginal people who lived and buried their ancestors there around 40,000 years ago.

Beauchamp Falls, Great Ocean Road, Otway Ranges, Victoria. From among the moss- and lichen-covered boulders some distance away, the rushing roar of the waterfall in the dense forest is somewhat subdued and ebbs away with the waters of the Aire River.

without recognising and respecting its natural limitations. While Australia's uniqueness — including the remarkable and irreplaceable endemicity of much of its flora and fauna — is better understood today, evidence of foreign influence is pervasive throughout the continent, in the most remote areas and in its densest settlements.

recreating the familiar

As in many 'Westernised' countries, the urban gardens of most Australian cities are designed around expanses of lush lawn, clusters of colourful roses and a plethora of other plants imported to impart a sense of the familiar. In some cooler, higher altitude townships of New South Wales' Blue Mountains, Victoria's Dandenong Ranges or South Australia's Mount Lofty Ranges, it is not uncommon to find cottage gardens complete with box hedges, hydrangeas and magnolias lovingly cultivated and pruned over decades but more appropriately found in the English Cotswolds. As well as private gardens, public streetscapes in cities like Sydney, Melbourne and Brisbane have also been adorned with imported trees and shrubs. Chinese elms, lantana, camphor laurel and exotic palms, among many others, were introduced for this purpose and have easily jumped the boundaries of the urban environment and invaded native ecosystems.

Well over 200 years down the track, native plants have found a much greater appreciation but are still considered inadequate by many who prefer the fragrant and colourful abundance of the lawns and gardens of their ancestral countries. Traditional summer rituals of hosing the garden — and the kids — at the end of a hot day are as familiar to Australians as Hills Hoist washing lines and barbecues. Only within the last decade or so have the rapid decline of freshwater resources and the increasingly unpredictable rainfall patterns across the continent served as a universal reminder of why predominantly temperate, water-loving plants are not at home on the driest continent on earth.

Like its urban environments, Australia's rural landscapes have been shaped by land-use ideals developed for soils and climates that Australia cannot offer. Two of the most essential ingredients for agriculture — good soils and reliable rain — are distinctly absent in most of Australia. A long geological history that included glaciation, droughts, floods, winds and weathering, coupled with very little soil-producing volcanic activity, left a continent largely unsuitable to the demands of modern land-use practices. Millions of years of erosion and deep chemical weathering of this ancient landmass resulted in a time-worn continent with only six per cent of soils of arable quality. Even the most basic preparation for agriculture — the clearing of land for pasture and cropping — that began immediately after the arrival of the earliest foreign settlers had unforeseen and detrimental consequences. Large parts of south-west Western Australia and eastern agricultural lands now bear the salty white scars where the removal of deep-rooted perennial vegetation led to a rise in groundwater and brought to the surface ancient salt deposits, permanently poisoning the ground to all but the most salt-tolerant vegetation. Damage has also been caused by the impact of pastoral practices on the landscape. The stocking and overgrazing of land by cattle, sheep and rabbits led to the erosion of the delicate topsoils that wash away in the rain or blow away in vast, ominous dust clouds during periods of drought. Large amounts of chemical fertilisers and pesticides are necessary to coax profitable yields from impoverished soils, and the downstream effects of chemical run-off include toxic algal blooms in ponds and waterways, and the decline of coral reefs due to excessive nutrient loads in streams that run into the sea. But hindsight is always perfect: none of these consequences were anticipated by those who arrived in the late 1800s with mouths to feed and hopes of new beginnings.

Quick sketches such as these illustrate that much of the modern Australian lifestyle originated elsewhere with the intention not to adapt to and appreciate what was on offer but to recreate what was safe and familiar. And after travelling many months on perilous journeys to an uncertain future, who could blame those hapless English souls that pulled into Botany Bay in 1788? After all, what in those days was known about the history of this continent and about the forces that had shaped it? Who would have thought of the unfamiliar shapes of its plants or the peculiar habits of its pouched mammals as indicators of the limitations of landscapes and climate? It would be many decades before Charles Darwin and Alfred Russel Wallace would inspire people to contemplate nature as the product of evolution and survival of the fittest, and even then the geological and climatic events that had shaped Australian landscapes over hundreds of millions of years would remain a mystery for a further century. Today, much more is known about the heritage of this country and some of the mystery has been solved. What has been revealed has added to the fascination with the ancient landscapes that once housed dinosaurs, and later giant wombats and kangaroos as well as antipodean marsupial lions and tigers, and continue to feature a unique array of life found nowhere else on earth.

Gondwana origins

The most defining characteristic of the shores that greeted the early settlers and all subsequent immigrants is that they are part of one of the oldest landmasses on earth. Integrated into the now legendary southern landmass of Gondwana, Australia was attached to Africa, Madagascar, South America,

▲ The thorny devil is well adapted to its desert environment. Despite its fearsome appearance, this remarkable desert-dweller is a threat only to small black ants, which make up its sole diet.

▶ Usually a vast expanse of dry red sand, the Sturt's Stony Desert in New South Wales comes to life after the rains. Within just a few days, ephemeral flowers like these poached-egg daisies shoot out of the ground and burst into bloom, putting on a spectacular display of life before drought once again claims this landscape.

Introduction: great southern land

India, Arabia, New Zealand, Antarctica and parts of South East Asia for over 200 million years. The shared ancestry of some of the fauna and flora of these continents is still apparent today. Gradually, Gondwana broke up, separating first Africa, then India and later New Zealand from the rest, and finally splitting Australia from its last connection to Antarctica about 45 million years ago. The remarkable age of the continent has been highlighted through discoveries such as that of a 4500 million-year-old zircon crystal embedded within a rock. The crystal dates back to 1000 million years before the earliest known forms of life and only 500 million years after the earth began to solidify from molten lava. Primeval rock still forms large surface areas of south-west Western Australia, the Northern Territory and parts of South Australia. Early volcanic activity over the next 1500 million years formed vast mountain ranges across the continent from Cape York across to south-west Western Australia. The erosion of these ranges over the millennia left behind massive blocks of sandstone that can still be seen in the Kimberley and Bungle Bungle regions of Western Australia and the Arnhem Plateau of the Northern Territory. By comparison, the majestic red sandstone of Uluru (Ayers Rock) and the conglomerate rock of the Kata Tjuta (The Olgas) were formed from eroded mountain sediments compressed by the sea only about 500 million years ago.

evolution of a continent

Australia is an ancient and stable landmass that was shaped over thousands of millions of years through cycles of sea level rises and recedences, continental rifting and stretching, emerging and eroding mountain chains and some volcanic activity. During this time, the emerging continent (still part of Gondwana) rotated up to 180 degrees through tectonic force and moved from north of the equator towards the South Pole. What is now Shark Bay in Western Australia, for example, once formed the very southern tip of the developing continent and was located just above the equator. One hundred and thirty million years later with the landmass twisted around 130 degrees, it was submerged at the north-western tip of Australia at 15 degrees North, while a further 140 million years on and still submerged, it formed the northernmost tip of the continent at 57 degrees South. What is now one evenly exposed continent was once a landmass of regions that were separated from each other by seaways for much of its development.

A basic understanding of the geological stages of Australia's development post-Gondwana is essential to appreciating the comparatively more recent land formations and the evolution of the plants and creatures that typify this country today. At the time of its final separation 45 million years ago, Australia was covered in rainforest and already home to a diversity of flowering plants, mammals and birds that had first begun to evolve 125 million years ago when a large range of invertebrates, amphibians and reptiles were already in existence. During the last 30 million years, climatic change came about through fluctuations in the growing Antarctic ice cap. These fluctuations caused sea levels and temperatures to rise and fall, and in the process produced changing environments conducive to the evolution of a vast variety of life. Warmer periods particularly yielded an abundance of fauna that included fish, frogs, turtles, lizards, snakes, bats and birds.

The warmer climate that occurred from 23.6 to 5.3 million years ago replaced the rainforest with temperate forest over south-eastern Australia. In Australia's central regions, the characteristic sandy and gibber (stony) deserts were still entirely absent and rainforest extended as far inland as Alice Springs. Volcanic activity along the Great Dividing Range (Great Divide), a section of land raised up during the separation of the New Zealand subcontinent over 80 million years ago, resulted from the northward drift of the continent over a hot-spot in the earth's crust and gave rise to patches of valuable fertile soil. In a land with ancient worn-out soil over most of its area, these soils became the foundations of a series of fertile basalt outcrops that support the forests of eastern Australia.

As the continent began to become drier around 15 million years ago, the beginnings of seasonal aridity favoured open and drier vegetation. As a consequence, fire caused by lightning found fuel and began to play an active role in shaping the environment. In parts of the east and south-east, rainforest was replaced by wet sclerophyll (hard-leaved) forest and grasslands. Central Australian fauna had by now diversified to include waterbirds like flamingos, and later eagles, cranes and frogmouths, and mammals such as early koalas, wombats, possums, macropods (the kangaroo family) and some carnivores.

A recurrence of warmer conditions with higher rainfall happened between 5.3 and 2.4 million years ago. In Western Australia, the increasing seasonality of the climate was marked by the evolution of a rich flora of two of Australia's most characteristic plant families, the Myrtaceae and Proteaceae. Banksias, dryandas, grevilleas, hakeas and casuarinas, as well as grasses, sedges and chenopods (salt-tolerant and drought-resistant forbs and shrubs such as saltbush) increased the distinct plant diversity of the west that was separated from the east of the continent by the Nullabor Plain. Meanwhile, the grasslands and chenopod shrublands that developed in the centre became home to the first grazing kangaroos.

The growing mass of Antarctic ice continued to control

Cape Wollamai, Phillip Island, Victoria, in stormy weather. The coastline of southern Australia is shaped by the cold currents that originate in Antarctica. Relentlessly battered by stormy seas, the shorelines are carved into jagged monuments and large round boulders.

Uluru–Kata Tjuta National Park, Northern Territory, at sunset. Meaning 'many heads' in local Aboriginal language, Kata Tjuta (The Olgas) rises out of flat desert country and is of great cultural significance to the Pitjantjatjara people.

14 **Introduction:** great southern land

global climates until the overall level of cooling resulted in the formation of the northern (Arctic) ice cap 2.4 million years ago. By now, the original dense Gondwanan vegetation had been reduced to mere remnants and rapid climate change led to the replacement of forests and woodlands with grasslands. Seasonal aridity, very windy conditions and high evaporation led to increased fire frequencies, and terrestrial organisms were forced to adapt rapidly to the challenges of these new environments. Sea-level fluctuations also continued to have a significant impact on the coasts of Australia. High sea levels between glaciation peaks led to limestone and salt depositions where the sea inundated the coastal fringes. Weathering and rapid change left central Australia highly arid, forcing the evolving flora and fauna such as wallabies and kangaroos, wombats, diprotodons (a wombat-like marsupial), hare-wallabies, and a range of carnivores including dasyurids (native cats) and the marsupial lion to once again adapt to dry and sparse conditions in an area that had been lush rainforest just a few million years earlier.

the impact of fire

From about 300,000 years ago, large areas of Australia had become as arid as they are today. Around 130,000 years ago, fossil records show that the increasing severity and frequency of lightning-caused fires required plants to evolve an increasing degree of fire tolerance. Regular fires meant that the diversity of flora generally decreased as the variety of fire-tolerant eucalypts increased. By now, the Australian soils that had once supported rainforests had become leached and weathered, and the absence of volcanic activity on most of the continent impaired the renewal of soils. Consequently, the biological limitations of sandy soils, salinity and high evaporation prevented significant vegetation changes when a wetter climate interval of around 5000 years brought brief relief to the aridity in many areas.

The last glacial stage between 20,000 and 18,000 years ago brought about an environmental crisis. While climates were twice as dry and windy as they are today, rainfall was considerably less than today and the extreme conditions were ideal for wildfires. For the Aborigines that had arrived by boat from the north and now called this continent home, times were hazardous and life was largely restricted to the edges of the country. Eighty per cent of the continent consisted of desert as sands blew wildly in the arid zones and formed the dune and gibber deserts we see today. When polar ice masses reached their maximum between 18,000 and 15,000 years ago, Australia faced its harshest and most defining drying period. Wide coastal plains resulted with the exposure of continental shelves, as sea levels dropped to 130 m (425 ft) below those of today. In the interglacial that followed, the modern-day continent developed many of its current vegetation features. These include the riparian forests that established along the river systems of the Murray basin as lowering water tables allowed deep-rooted trees to become established.

Between 14,000 and 10,000 years ago, rising sea levels separated the islands to the north of Australia including New Guinea, flooded the Gulf of Carpentaria and created the Arafura Sea. To the south, Bass Strait became inundated and separated Tasmania from the rest of the continent. The next 10,000 years saw a tempering of the climate that made it more favourable for modern plants and animals. Temperature variations became less extreme and winds less harsh. Fire in the deserts continued to force the decline of trees, shrubs, grasses and sedges in favour of ephemerals that are able to weather fires and reemerge in burnt areas.

Along coastal areas, changes in rainfall patterns played a large part in shaping the vegetation. Favoured by wetter conditions, karri (a type of eucalypt) forest had spread over large areas of the south-west of Western Australia by 8000 years ago, and competed with other eucalypts such as jarrah and marri. Over time the ratio of karri to jarrah and marri forests continued to be determined by rainfall. Around the same time in south-east Australia, woodlands and forests, replaced by open vegetation and confined to smaller refuges during the recent glacial, once again spread into their former ranges except where constrained by physical obstacles such as sand dunes and other barriers that had formed in the meantime. By about 5000 years ago, Australia's major regions and their plants and animals looked like they do today. Fires remained the key factor influencing the landscapes and resulted in a continued selection for fire-tolerant species and the loss of fire-vulnerable plants.

Despite its long separation from the supercontinent of Gondwana, almost all of Australia's plants and animals originated before the continent had broken away. Plant groups such as the cycads, tree ferns, ferns and most of the early flowering plants all had their origins in Gondwana and some underwent further evolution on the newly separated continent. Rainforest remnants that have persisted throughout remain almost unchanged after 60 million years, while eucalypts and other sclerophyllous plants that had evolved to suit the poor soils were favoured further by the pressure of fire.

monotremes and marsupials

The best illustration of how the physical isolation of Australia led to the retention of early evolutionary characteristics and eliminated the influences that led to the evolution of a different fauna elsewhere is found among Australia's mammals. Around the world, the three main evolutionary groups of mammals — monotremes, marsupials and placental mammals — can be placed along a continuum from early to more recently evolved. In simple terms, evolution is a long-term response to external pressures (changes) such as climate, predators, habitat changes and competition with other species. In combination, these pressures drive the development of whatever characteristics or strategies are needed for a species to continue to survive in the emerging environment. The more pressure exists, the more rapidly living organisms evolve; fewer pressures and a more stable environment result in a slower rate of evolution. The earliest evolved living group of mammals is the monotremes, which lay eggs, do not have teats and instead suckle their young from ducts called hotspots on their abdomen. Monotremes (echidnas and platypus) lay soft-shelled eggs, and the subsequent development of the young outside of the female's body carries considerable risks to the young by exposing them to external threats at a very vulnerable stage of development. A more evolved version of this basic reproductive design is that of the marsupials (such as the kangaroo family), which give birth to extremely underdeveloped young but have pouches with internal teats in which the young can continue to develop in relative safety. Kangaroos are also able to control their breeding and delay the development of embryos during times of tough environmental conditions. The most modern version of the female reproductive system is that of placental mammals, which allows young to develop to an advanced stage *in utero* before birth. While this strategy proved most successful in response to changes in other parts of the world, monotremes and two-thirds of all living marsupials (e.g., kangaroos, koalas, possums) remain only in Australia and nearby New Guinea, while the remainder of marsupials (e.g., opossums) occur in South America. Three orders of placental mammals — rodents, bats and seals — are also present in Australia, but while seals occur throughout the southern oceans, the first two evolved elsewhere and arrived via New Guinea across the relatively narrow Torres Strait.

Australia's marsupials come in a large range of shapes and sizes. From the tiny feathertail glider to the big red kangaroo, they fill the breadth of habitat niches in the spectrum of terrestrial landscapes — wet and dry forests, open woodlands, shrubby heath, rocky plateaus, grasslands, deserts and savannas. Some are meat-eaters (e.g., quolls, Tasmanian devils and marsupial moles), some like a mixed menu of plants and insects (e.g., bandicoots), some are broadly vegetarian (e.g., koalas, possums and kangaroos) and others rely on flowers (ringtail possums), nectar and pollen (gliders), fruit (musky rat-kangaroo) and fungi, bulbs and tubers (potoroos and bettongs) in their diet to survive. Despite this great diversity, there is a distinct absence of large predators among Australia's native wildlife. While Australia once had a marsupial lion that ruled the hierarchy of predators, the largest and most intriguing predator in modern times (until around 3000 years ago on the mainland) was the wolf-like Tasmanian tiger or thylacine. Together with its contemporary, the Tasmanian devil, the tiger roamed in much of Australia's open forests and woodlands until the arrival of the dingo from Asia about 4000 years ago increased the competition for the tiger's food resources. Both tigers and devils remained in dingo-free Tasmania until the tiger was hunted to extinction by white settlers last century. The last tiger, captive in a Hobart Zoo, died in 1936.

The relative scarcity of mammalian predators on the Australian mainland even prior to the demise of tigers and devils meant that there was little threat of predation for the many ground-dwelling marsupials found throughout the country. While the upper ranks of the food chain were occupied by raptors and larger reptiles such as snakes and crocodiles, their impact was tempered by the natural system they were part of. This came to an abrupt end 200 years ago with the arrival of European settlers and their companions — dogs, cats and foxes. Naïve to the stealth and speed of these predators, Australia's frog, reptile, bird and small to medium-sized marsupial fauna were easy pickings for the new arrivals. Once these predators became widespread, many species were unable to withstand the hunting pressure and their numbers declined dramatically. In addition to new predators, the introduction of rabbits, pigs and hard-hooved stock such as cattle, horses and donkeys had a devastating impact on fragile soils and vegetation, and many native species lost the competition for resources. Combined with the impacts of land-clearing, well over 100 plant and animal species have become extinct since modern settlement and thousands of others have declined, some to dangerously low numbers.

recent arrivals

While Australia's fauna and flora took shape over millions of years, the arrival and influence of humans on the continent is only a recent event. Although not entirely resolved, it is certain that Aborigines had arrived via northern lands by at least 40,000–60,000 years ago and possibly as early as 140,000 years ago. Before European colonisation, over 700 different Aboriginal language groups are thought to have existed across the continent. The many languages and dialects served as cultural communication tools that also helped to identify the speakers' belonging to the traditional lands on which each language was spoken. The impact of Aboriginal people on the landscape was considered significant by some

Fern tree gully, Tarra Bulge National Park, Victoria.

Hills with spinifex grass at sunrise, Millstream-Chichester National Park, Western Australia. The undulating hills of the Pilbara region are a cache of mineral treasures. Beneath the spinifex country, iron ore is one of the predominant riches that is mined from the characteristic red rock.

Introduction: great southern land

until the impact of Europeans in a mere 200 years gave new meaning to the term 'significant'. The critical difference between the two was that Aboriginal people were largely nomadic, moving across the land as hunter-gatherers, while Europeans had been sedentary since the development of early agriculture and subsequent technology. With hindsight, the advantages of nomadism over permanent settlement on a continent fundamentally constrained in its ability to yield food seem obvious and eminently sensible. The survival of Aboriginal people was directly dependent on maintaining the land that sustained them and taking from it only what it could readily offer. 'Looking after country', part of the Aboriginal ethos that enabled their survival, required a deep fundamental understanding of natural history: the landscapes and seasons, the yielding patterns of plants (e.g., flowering and fruiting) and the life cycles and behaviours of animals that were crucial to their immediate as well as to future survival. Aboriginal 'traditional ecological knowledge' therefore provided the foundation for a spiritual philosophy that governed the rules of human behaviour to ensure the protection of the land.

custodians of the land

Despite their adaptability, it is likely that the continued presence of Aboriginal people over time had some effect on the landscape. Different schools of thought attribute varying degrees of responsibility to Australia's indigenous people with respect to two main landscape changes — the disappearance of Australia's megafauna, and the permanent alteration of vegetation as a result of active fire management. The first assertion, that Aborigines over-hunted the large fauna and caused their extinction, is based on species losses around the time and after the likely arrival of the first Aborigines in Australia between 40,000 and 60,000 years ago. Some extinction occurred around 40,000 years ago, while other species of megafauna, including some of the giant kangaroos, giant rat-kangaroos, the diprotodon (a precursor to modern wombats) and the marsupial lion disappeared from the fossil record after about 20,000 years ago. One recent hypothesis suggests that these represented predominantly the larger and slower species or those in direct competition with humans, and that they were easy to hunt as they were naïve to humans as predators. Another school of thought, however, discounts the likelihood of over-hunting as a key extinction cause and attributes the disappearance of the megafauna to climatic changes such as those that brought about the extreme conditions of the last glacial stage around 20,000–18,000 years ago.

The second major impact attributed by some to Aboriginal people occurred through the practice of fire-stick farming. Although wildfire had been a part of the Australian environment since the late Miocene epoch (i.e., more than 5.3 million years ago), Aborigines began to use fire to their advantage by deliberately burning patches of land to flush out wildlife and to generate a fresh supply of green feed for themselves and for the mammals they hunted. Typically, only smallish patches were set alight with 'cool' burns, leaving adjacent areas unburnt and intact as refuges. These patch burns were generally conducted late in the dry season and had the simultaneous effects of reducing the build-up of fuel in the landscapes and creating firebreaks that helped to contain the violent and highly damaging wildfires. The long-term impact of this fire-management strategy and the increased frequency of fires, however, is postulated to have caused a gradual change in the vegetation structure of the burnt landscapes from fire-sensitive species such as cool temperate forests to fire-tolerant species such as eucalypts, many of which benefit from occasional fire to help with the germination of their seeds. A second theory attributes the rise of eucalypts and other sclerophyllous plants directly to the limitations of poor soils and once again discounts the impact of Aboriginal people on broad-scale vegetation change.

Irrespective of these debates, the Aboriginal ethic of nurturing the land and considering themselves an integral part of the landscape enabled their largely harmonious co-existence with nature over tens of thousands of years. Between 250,000 and 750,000 Aborigines of perhaps more than 500 cultural groups lived in Australia before European arrival and passed on traditional ways and knowledge through generations. Many travelled along particular 'songlines', which are old, established but unmarked routes across the country along which traditional rituals and activities were conducted and which crossed with other songlines to bring about contact between language groups. The term songlines refers to the Aboriginal belief that all features of the landscapes were called up from beneath the ground by ancestral spirits through song. The location and significance of sections of these songlines were passed on between generations and created a rich cultural tapestry that endured over many thousands of years.

Today, Aboriginal numbers have dwindled to less than one per cent of the total Australian population, and their cultures have been marginalised by the manifestations of modern civilisation — permanent townships, cultivated and manufactured food — that have undermined the need to impart traditional knowledge to new generations. No longer hunter-gatherers, many now suffer from carbohydrate-rich diets that their bodies are not accustomed to; diabetes is a common disease, and the average lifespan of an Aboriginal person is considerably shorter than that of 'whitefellas'. Ironically, as environmental problems caused by inappropriate land management have become increasingly apparent, the value of Aboriginal wisdom and their innate understanding of the country have found renewed appreciation and are increasingly being utilised to help restore and manage altered parts of the land. Particularly in arid regions where native species and ecosystems are threatened by feral animals such as rabbits, camels and foxes, by agricultural weeds such as buffel grass, and by poorly managed fires, and where existing wildlife is notoriously cryptic and difficult to detect, the remarkable Aboriginal skills of reading every minute aspect of the landscape, including signs of life patently invisible to non-indigenous people, are helping to establish the presence or absence of species and form the basis for management plans to ensure their survival. Barely discernible tracks in the desert sand reveal the presence of a legless lizard, a thorny devil or a mulgara (a small, rodent-like marsupial); the condition of a scat (dropping) provides information about the animal that left it, what it ate, its general condition and how long ago it passed the spot where the scat is found. Some species such as lizards or the marsupial mole leave no apparent trace at all, and only strategic digging — at a site plainly obvious to no one but a local — will uncover their presence. Given the vastness of the range, finding the proverbial needle in a haystack seems like a fairer challenge.

a fragile diversity

Despite the graphic depictions of history as provided by geologists, palaeontologists and historians, it is almost impossible to imagine the immense forces of nature that shaped the vast continent that is Australia as we know it at this moment in time — the lush forests of tropical North Queensland, living remnant of Gondwana; the extensive ranges of the Great Divide, boosted in sections by volcanic activity to create the fertile stretch of land along the east coast; the forests, woodlands and grasslands so characteristic of eastern and western Australia, shaped by drought, fire and rain; the arid red centre, featuring Uluru and Kata Tjuta (The Olgas), weathered remnants of an ancient mountain range; Western Australia's south-west, isolated by vast expanses of desert and home to the most endemic fauna and flora; the northern savannas and the wetlands of Kakadu and the Kimberley, seasonal havens for a rich diversity of wildlife. An awareness of the processes of the continent's creation from its Gondwanan origins, the limited soil-creating volcanic activity and the effects of repeated periods of flooding and drying, tropical and glacial climates, winds and fires and the associated weathering of soils and landscapes is essential to appreciating the glorious diversity of life — plants, animals and the systems they are a part of — that carefully evolved to suit just such a harsh backdrop and to fill each niche of the landscape, no matter how apparently inhospitable.

In the 21st century, Australia's landscapes face new challenges. After millennia of evolution, the pressure placed on the planet by the inundation of people is taking its toll. Excessive resource consumption, pollution and human-induced climate change are affecting all living systems, and Australia's are no exception. As illustrated throughout this book, water is of critical importance to even the hardiest parts of the continent; its absence profoundly affects the life cycle of all living organisms. Changing rainfall patterns and temperature ranges, along with the overuse of our limited freshwater resources, are posing serious threats to the future of many of Australia's ecosystems. Combined with the additional pressure of invasive weeds and feral animal incursions, unsuitable agriculture and the increased likelihood of wildfires and tropical cyclones, the Australian continent is undergoing significant changes that will relegate many of its icons to history within the current century. How many is up to us — more than ever, the future is in our hands. Acting now will ensure that the beautiful images on these pages remain true to life instead of becoming lamentable memories.

At the end of a stormy day, the retreating tempest leaves the rugged shores of Cape Conran Coastal Park, Victoria, in tranquil shades of pink and lilac.

The imposing limestone walls that border Windjana Gorge, Western Australia, are the remnants of an ancient reef whose waters have long since ebbed away. Pink mulla mulla flowers, ephemeral and dependent on moisture, are evidence of recent rain.

Introduction: great southern land

In the dry interior of the country, these eucalypts occupy a prime position on the edge of Big Ellery Hole, a permanent waterhole in the West MacDonnell Ranges.

Bell Gorge, Kimberley, Western Australia at sunset. Bell Gorge is one of the most spectacular gorges of the Kimberley region. Through a series of cascading waterfalls and pools, the creek drops over 100 m (328 ft) into the dark pool that reflects the gathering clouds in this image.

At up tp 5 m (15 ft) in length, the amethyst or scrub python is Australia's largest snake. It occurs only along the eastern coast from Townsville to Cape York Peninsula and preys on mammals that may include large wallabies and tree kangaroos.

London Bridge, Port Campbell National Park, Victoria, at dusk. Battered by the ocean over millions of years, the limestone arch to which this coastal landmark on the Great Ocean Road owed its name finally surrendered to the ocean in 1990. Dramatic changes like these are reminders that Australia's ancient landscapes are fragile and continue to be shaped by the elements.

Eastern grey kangaroo with joey in pouch. Kangaroos and wallabies are widespread throughout Australia; as marsupials, they owe their success to a range of biological, physiological and behavioural adaptations to an often harsh and unpredictable climate.

Beyond the Horizon

Western Australia

Of the six states and two territories created by the mid 19th century to divide the country into governable portions, Western Australia's 2.5 million square kilometres (965,255 square miles) take up no less than one-third of the continent. The fact that only about one-tenth of Australia's population lives in this state is indicative of the size of the deserts the drying of the continent created in Western Australia and the interior of the country.

Deserts comprise the vast majority of Western Australia and have isolated the south-west of the state as the most temperate and habitable region. While parts of the eastern states benefited greatly from volcanic activity, similar soil-enriching processes were distinctly absent in the west. Here, the landscapes were shaped by millennia of sedimentation as sea levels rose and fell and large parts of the land were periodically inundated by the ocean. In the south-east of the state, the rising limestone seabed created the flat and treeless Nullabor Plain that sustains little more than saltbush and other shrubs. To the south, the Nullabor is bordered by sheer cliffs and open ocean, to the north by the scrub-covered dunes of the Great Victoria Desert. Other deserts stretch throughout the interior, extending to the rugged and rocky Pilbara region in the west, and the tropical savannas of the Kimberley in the north of the state. Throughout most of Western Australia, the desert climate brings with it hot, dry summers and mild but equally dry winters, with an average yearly rainfall of less than 250 mm (10 in). Marble Bar, a town on the eastern fringe of the Pilbara, lays claim to being the hottest place in Australia; temperatures of more than 40°C (104°F) are common for many months of the year and the hottest day to date was recorded in 1905 when the mercury soared to a staggering 49.1°C (120°F)! Along the coast, however, the harsh aridity of the deserts is tempered by reasonable coastal rainfall and generally milder conditions that accommodate a great diversity of life. The south-west corner of the state especially benefits from a Mediterranean climate where relatively higher winter rainfall and cooler temperatures compensate somewhat for the hot and dry summer months and poor soils. However, these western coastal regions have found themselves completely isolated by the surrounding interior deserts that form a formidable barrier to possible incursions of plants and animals from the east of the country. This isolation gave rise to the evolution of a distinct and unique flora and fauna, and over time produced a richness and endemicity (uniqueness) of species that now sees Western Australia's South West Botanical Province recognised as being

The absence of sharp edges in the sandstone landscapes of Purnululu National Park attests to the smoothing forces of wind and water over many millions of years. It's the end of the dry season, and the rains of the wet will soon fill this creek and continue the task of slowly carving out its bedrock.

Karri tree forest in morning fog, Warren National Park. Once heavily logged for their timbers, karri trees are among the most iconic and spectacular eucalypts of south-west Western Australia.

of conservation significance at a global scale. Approximately 80 per cent of south-west Western Australia's plant and animal species are considered endemic and are therefore found nowhere else on earth.

The vast distances between the habitable east and west coasts and the harsh interior that separates them also ensured that Western Australia remained a remote and largely unknown terrain to Europeans long after the east had been settled. Although two small English settlements had been established near Albany in 1826 and along the Swan River (later Perth) in 1829, for a number of decades after colonisation settlers from elsewhere on the continent could only travel there by ship as no overland route yet existed. To challenge this obstacle, in 1841 Edward John Eyre and a party of four men commenced an overland expedition from South Australia in an attempt (his second) to establish the feasibility of a coastal stock route between Adelaide and Albany. Blistering heat and the torment of blood-sucking flies made the journey slow and laborious, and a lack of food and water forced the group to capture dew for drinking and to slaughter one of their valuable horses for food. After losing three men through murder and desertion, an exhausted Eyre and his remaining Aboriginal companion did finally arrive in Albany after a long five months, only to conclude that a stock route to the west was definitely out of the question.

One of the most distinguishing natural features of Western Australia is the spectacularly colourful abundance of its wildflowers, particularly in the wetter, near-coastal regions. From the brightest reds and yellows to the spectrum of delicate pastel pinks, striking blues, lilacs, oranges and the deepest purples, the south-west corner alone is adorned with over 6000 different flowering plants that spring to life after the winter rains. Orchids are well represented, as is the Myrtaceae family that includes the eucalypts, bottlebrushes, grevilleas and paperbark trees; Proteaceae such as dryandras, hakeas, grevilleas and banksias; and Papilionaceae, which includes the acacias. Most plants occur in heathland or woodland communities and are well adapted to predominantly sandy and drought-prone soils. Winter rains can bring on a profusion of colourful blooms within only a couple of days, dressing the landscape in a floral abundance that varies from the traditional to the bizarre. A characteristic shared by several plant families is the slender and delicate tendril structure of their flowers. Grevilleas, banksias and coneflowers especially consist of loose spikes or dense clusters of straight, gently curved or hooked petals that entice insects, birds and small nectar-loving mammals like the tiny honey possum. Other flowers, like those of the shaggy dryandra that grows in the heathlands of the north coast or the small fringe lilies of the south-west jarrah forests, are fringed by feather-like 'bracts' that nod and sway at the whim of a breeze. Even the traditionally white or cream-coloured eucalypt blossoms make an exception in the west, where several types of gum trees, including the red-flowering gum and the mottlecah, colloquially known as the 'Rose of the West', produce vibrant red and orange flowers. Among all the multi-hued abundance of flowers that grow from ground to canopy level, perhaps the most bizarre are the striking kangaroo paws. While the plants themselves are low-growing clumps of elongated leaves, the flowering stems can reach up to 1.5 m (5 ft) and their oddly-shaped, velvety flowers are situated towards the tip of each stem. Once a blossom has burst open, it bears an uncanny resemblance to the stunted four-clawed front limb of a kangaroo. Flora seems to pay homage to fauna as the kangaroo paws' stems and flowers even have a coating of fine 'fur' that serves to trap air and thereby reduces evaporation.

the south-west: 'land of giants'

Somewhat less colourful but no less impressive than the wildflowers of the woodlands and heaths are the endemic tall eucalypt forests of the south-west. The Mediterranean climate, acidic gravelly soils and good winter rainfall of the south-west's near-coastal region supports several distinctive tree species that thrive in these conditions and give the region a unique character. In this 'land of the giants', size is of the essence — admiring the massive canopy of the south-west karri forest from the distant ground is a humbling experience for a tiny human! Of several iconic eucalypt species, karri is by far the most imposing and competes only with the amazing mountain ash of Australia's south-eastern forests for the status of tallest flowering hardwood in the world. Karri trees can grow up to 90 m (295 ft) tall and take almost 100 years to reach this height before redirecting their energy to producing a solid girth. A multitude of branches spread outwards from smooth, straight trunks and accommodate a profusion of white flowers. A single mature karri may produce 500,000 flowers in a summer season and its value to nectar-seeking wildlife is unequalled — it can yield up to a massive 250 kg (550 lbs) of honey!

Slightly smaller than the karri trees, marri trees or redgums are another equally distinctive eucalypt species of these forests. Rooted in pockets of good soils and in ample space, individual marri trees may grow up to 45 m (147 ft) tall and develop a broad, shade-bearing crown of leaves. However, the marri trait of adaptability also sees it in good stead in more variable conditions and marginal landscapes. On poor, sandy coastal soils, the marri foregoes its regal stature and takes on a short, gnarled form better suited to the tougher conditions. Thanks to its size and shape, in good conditions the marri has a spectacular flowering habit, and when in bloom, masses of oversized, cream-coloured blossoms at the tips of its branches can give the marri the appearance of a massive cauliflower. The honey-scented nectar is relished by birds, possums and insects, and the marri's gumnuts are a staple for Western Australia's magnificent Carnaby's and red-tailed black cockatoos.

Another distinctive tree species of the south west forests is the jarrah. At a mere 30 to 40 m (98–130 ft) in height on good soils, jarrah is a smaller tree compared with karri and marri trees and often grows in mixed forest with the latter. Like karri, jarrah is a hardwood whose dense timber is termite resistant and a prized material for buildings and furniture. Old-growth jarrah forests have been logged extensively since the 1860s and much of the timber was exported interstate and overseas. While extensive jarrah forest still abounds, little of it is 'old growth'.

These days, a more insidious threat to jarrah communities than logging is that of Phytophthora dieback, a disease caused by an invasive, root-rot causing fungus. While both marri and karri are resistant to this fungus, jarrah naturally hosts a suite of root fungi that increase its vulnerability to the dieback fungus. Dieback was accidentally introduced following European settlement, probably via plants imported from Asia. The spores are carried in the soil and their easy transfer has made it a key threat to the forest ecosystems of the wetter regions of south-west Western Australia, although other types of dieback also occur in forests along the east coast. As many as 40 per cent of the south-west's flowering plants are susceptible to dieback; once infected with the fungus, a plant becomes unable to absorb enough water and dies. Dieback is not eradicable, although it can be partially managed by phosphite chemical treatment. Stringently managing the inadvertent spread of dieback-infected soil during activities such as road building and maintenance, timber harvesting, bushwalking and via the nursery trade have proved the best ways of controlling it.

Although heavily impacted by dieback as well as by salinisation, fire, fragmentation and climate change and dependent on careful management, the south-west represents the most fertile area in a very dry state and is home to an array of amazing wildlife. Seen in a national context, the wildlife of the west generally distinguishes itself as much by the species that do not occur here as by those that do. The most obvious omissions in the south-west are koalas, platypus and flying foxes. While there is no evidence of platypus ever occurring in the west, fossil remains of modern koalas estimated at around 30,000 years old have been found in caves south of Perth and along the southern edge of the Nullabor Plain. Their disappearance has been variously attributed to rapid environmental change or to Aboriginal hunting. Two species of flying fox, the black and little red flying fox, do occur in Western Australia but mostly in the wetter Kimberley region and only extend as far south as to around Shark Bay. As there are no fossil records of flying foxes in Australia, it is likely that they are only relatively recent colonists from a time when New Guinea and Australia were connected (up to around 20,000 years ago) and that they simply never advanced to the south-west forests.

vulnerable and unique

But despite these charismatic omissions, the south-west of the continent has some fascinating wildlife of its own. One sprightly inhabitant that forages for termites among the jarrah and wandoo (another type of eucalypt endemic to Western Australia) forests and woodlands is the numbat. Resembling a tiny African aardvark with its elongate snout and long, flicking tongue, a squirrel with its frenetic movements, and the extinct Tasmanian tiger with its black-and-white-striped back and straight tail, the numbat is — remarkably — the only marsupial that specialises exclusively in a diet of termites. Given the abundance of termites in Australia, the lack of competition for this food has meant that the numbat has not needed any special foraging adaptations such as limbs for digging into termite mounds. It simply searches among leaf litter and dead branches and uses its acute sense of smell and clawed forefeet to uncover its favourite food, consuming about 20,000 termites per day. One particular characteristic does, however, set it apart from the majority of other small marsupials — in accordance with the diurnal (daytime) activity pattern of its prey, the numbat forages by day and sleeps at night, making it the only Australian mammal that is active only by day.

The small range of the numbat in the forests south-east of Perth makes it extremely vulnerable to the threat of introduced predators such as foxes and cats and it relies on careful conservation management to survive. This also applies to a number of other species that once had much larger distributions but are now found only in small pockets within the south-west. Two of the nations most threatened are the small, truffle-loving Gilbert's potoroo and the western swamp tortoise. The fate of Gilbert's potoroo is most precarious; only rediscovered in 1994 after it had been thought to be extinct for over 80 years, its total wild population is restricted to two sites on the south coast and numbers around 30 individuals. Like the numbat, this ground-dwelling marsupial is vulnerable to fox and cat predation as well as to wildfire within its tiny habitat. Its preferred food of root-fungi also makes it sensitive to the effects of dieback disease which destroys the root systems that are its foraging grounds. The western swamp tortoise is similarly restricted to just two enclosed swamp sites near Perth and has been reduced to a population of less than 100 individuals. Considered to be one of the world's

Purnululu or Bungle Bungles at sunrise, Purnululu National Park. The horizontal tiger stripes of these weathered 'beehive' rock formations comprise alternate layers of orange silica and dark-green lichen. Worn down to its current shape over a period of 20 million years, Purnululu is fragile and evidence of ongoing erosion is clearly visible.

rarest reptiles, it has been severely impacted by encroaching agriculture, urbanisation and predation by foxes. All are now kept at bay by tall, electrified fences, and tortoises successfully bred in captivity are released into these predator-proof 'exclosures' to allow these critically endangered reptiles to survive in their native habitat.

the sea's legacy

Beyond the south-west, the geological history of Western Australia and the legacy of sand and limestone deposits left by millennia of sea-level changes pervades the landscapes throughout the state. To the north of Perth, the Pinnacles Desert in the Nambung National Park is a monument to those formative periods. Among flat expanses of yellow sand offset by a luminous blue sky, the Pinnacles consist of a landscape of odd-shaped limestone pillars that randomly poke out of the ground and range in height from a few centimetres to over 5 m (16 ft). The sandy indentations from which some pillars emerge suggest that they were recently dropped out of the sky, but the spires of the Pinnacles are actually the visible tips of a hidden world below. The structures formed when ancient sands enriched with the lime from broken seashells became calcified and, gradually eroded by wind and sand over about 30,000 years, left just the hardiest remnants exposed to the elements. Some look like an odd assemblage of tombstones complete with an authentic covering of lichen, perhaps commemorating the millions of shells that posthumously contributed to their making. Ominously, groups of Pinnacles appear and disappear over time as the sands shift to cover those in the south and uncover others still hidden beneath the northern parts of the desert.

In the waters of the mid-western coast, Carnarvon and the Shark Bay World Heritage Area draw attention away from terrestrial landscapes of marine origins to marine landscapes that feature modern life. The diversity of aquatic life in and around Shark Bay ensured that it was occupied by Aborigines at least as early as 22,000 years ago. After an initial visit by the Dutch explorer Dirk Hartog in 1616, the bay was named by William Dampier in 1699 after the abundance of sharks he spotted there. Sharks mingle with dolphins and green and leatherback turtles in its pristine blue waters, while humpback whales intermittently pass by on their migrations to seasonal feeding grounds and occasionally use the bay as a convenient stopover. Among the most unusual and precious inhabitants of Shark Bay, however, are the herds of dugongs that graze on the many types of seagrasses that grow throughout the 4000 square kilometres (1545 square miles) of the bay area; the shallow beds of the Wooramel seagrass bank are the largest in the world and comprise only a part of what's on offer.

Unlike seals and sea lions, dugongs are the only herbivorous mammals that spend their entire life in the ocean. Dugongs live in shallow, warm, subtropical and tropical coastal waters, and Shark Bay is at the southernmost end of their west coast distribution in Australia. Like whales and dolphins, dugongs have a horizontal tail fluke to propel their large, rotund frame through the seagrass meadows, and their solid bone structure and downward-facing, velvet-lipped snouts are perfectly suited for browsing on the sea bed. In a less buoyant environment, the generous proportions of a 400-kg (880-lb) dugong would make it cumbersome and awkward; beneath the ocean surface, however, it moves elegantly and with an air of sedate calm that belies its naturally curious nature that is supported by excellent hearing and good eyesight.

Like the dugongs, the bottlenose dolphins that share the pristine waters of Shark Bay are also slow breeders and carry their young for 12 months before giving birth. The long pregnancies ensure that the young are well-developed at birth and can fend for themselves in the unpredictable ocean environment, encouraged by the watchful proximity of their mothers. Dolphins have a popular reputation for playfulness, and their wave-riding habits and energetic aerial acrobatics are often admired as displays of joyous exuberance. In the shallow waters of Monkey Mia on the western shore of Shark Bay, the social bottlenose dolphins have become so accustomed to humans that they regularly swing by for a morning visit. The privilege of an encounter with a wild dolphin is an unforgettable experience as, for a brief moment in time, two highly intelligent species connect across the unconquerable divide of their separate worlds. Bottlenose dolphins use echolocation and a complex repertoire of whistles, clicks and squeaks to communicate with their pod. While they do not have a sense of smell, their hearing is outstanding and at an upper range of 100 kilohertz, about four times more acute than that of humans. The calm, appraising gaze of these remarkable mammals is strangely familiar and leaves a lasting sense that the planet's most intelligent creatures do not live on land.

While much of Shark Bay's magic is found in the sea, its shore holds a few surprises of its own. One is Shell Beach, a sparkling white stretch of shoreline that consists of more than 100 km (62 miles) of tiny shells up to 10 m (32 ft) deep. The shells were deposited over thousands of years in a process that is still unclear to science. Marine and land environments have literally become one as in places the shells are so tightly packed that they form a solid mass

◀◀ Karijini (formerly Hamersley Range) National Park in the Pilbara, is one of the hottest parts of the country. The stunning gorges and pools that are found in this area provide welcome relief from the heat.

During the dry season, northern rivers like the Pentecost look inviting to fishers and swimmers. Looks can be deceiving however. Saltwater crocodiles often inhabit these waters and are not generously disposed to intruders.

Wild Australia

One of the jewels of the West Australian coast, Cape Peron is a vantage point from which to spot turtles, dugongs, rays and dolphins that frequent the World Heritage-listed Shark Bay.

that is used as building material in nearby towns. Perhaps the most mind-boggling feature of Shark Bay, however, is contained in an isolated pool at the southern end of the bay. What at first glance looks unremarkably like scattered rocks in the shallow water is actually an aggregation of living stromatolites. Not unlike modern coral reefs, stromatolites are associations between primitive cyanobacteria and algae that work together to bind ocean sediments and sand into structures that eventually become hard rock. But there is much more to these unassuming structures than meets the eye. Stromatolites evolved over 3.5 billion years and initiated the most fundamental process necessary for complex life to evolve — the production of oxygen through photosynthesis. Stromatolites photosynthesise in sunlight, using carbon dioxide and water to produce oxygen. Living stromatolites require the clear water and hypersaline conditions found at Hamelin Pool to thrive undisturbed by other organisms that cannot tolerate the high salt levels. To observe these innocuous looking 'rocks' and appreciate the critical role they played in enabling productive life is to mark a critical milestone in the business plan for planet earth: oxygen? Tick. Next challenge: things that breathe.

hidden treasures

In coastal Western Australia, the rich bounty of the Indian Ocean competes favourably with that offered by the geology of the land. Fishing and pearling industries along the central and north coasts have compensated for the poor agricultural yields of a landscape whose soils were only ever marginally suited to pastoralism. To seafaring explorers, the rocky west coast often proved hostile and the remnants of several Dutch wrecks from the 17th and 18th centuries mingle with others that have met their fate in more recent times. But calamitous to one person is spectacular to another — the massive cliffs of Kalbarri to the south of Shark Bay and the rocky shores of the Carnarvon Coast embody some of the rugged beauty Western Australia is so much admired for.

For all its biological wonders, Western Australia keeps many of its treasures hidden from view. This is a state where geology matters and nowhere more so than in the mineral-rich Pilbara region. Over half a million square kilometres (193,000 square miles), the Pilbara sits on an eroded block of land more than 2.8 billion years old. The vast Pilbara features three distinct landscapes: a sprawling coastal plain, the red rocky inland ranges, and the arid deserts that extend into the centre of the continent. The abundance of marine life in the rich coastal waters provides a stark contrast to the barren terrestrial landscapes it borders. Ningaloo Marine Park which surrounds the jutting land-tongue of North West Cape is a harbour of marine riches that were appreciated and utilised by Aboriginal people as long as 34,000 years ago. Like Shark Bay, the magnificent Ningaloo Reef provides a habitat for marine turtles, dugongs and manta rays, and the seagrasses and corals are home to a myriad of rainbow-coloured fish. The submarine environment seems to create only the boldest exhibitionists who appear to compete for the titles of 'most outrageous body colour' and 'most ludicrous shape', with many outstanding candidates in both categories. Along the shore, the mood is more sedate as seabirds such as pied oystercatchers and gannets prefer a theme of black, white and pale grey, occasionally offset by a red bill, yellow eyes or blue feet. In the crystal-clear turquoise waters, however, the most breathtaking inhabitant by far is the massive, slow-moving whale shark, the largest fish on earth. This huge and whimsically polka-dotted filter-feeder cruises slowly across oceanic currents, straining water through a mesh of spongy tissue between its gills to extract plankton and masses of small fish to fuel its 40-tonne (39-ton) body. The whale sharks' annual visits to Ningaloo coincide with the spectacular coral-spawning season in autumn when minute planktonic marine life is in abundance and krill congregate *en masse* to gorge themselves on this bounty. Despite their enormous size, whale sharks have been known to 'hang' vertically above the clouds of krill, seeming to surreptitiously 'inhale' their meal from above.

Inland from the shore and coastal plain, the deep rusty reds of the ranges form a vivid backdrop to the pale grasses and the smatterings of stunted shrubs and trees that eke out a living from the harsh ground. Karijini (formerly Hamersley Range) National Park typifies this dry, barren landscape with its hilly ridges and its magnificently coloured gorges, etched through hundreds of layers of ancient sediment. Among the vast semi-arid and arid landscapes of Western Australia, the gorges of the Pilbara Ranges are invaluable oases for plant and animal life and have been formally recognised as unique refuges. Fed by precious stream water, the gorges' lush, green and sheltered environment supports a diversity of vegetation that includes the familiar eucalypt and paperbark trees and the rarer Livistona and Millstream fan palms.

Elsewhere, away from prying eyes, threatened wildlife occupies all possible niches — black-footed rock wallabies scamper over stony ridges, carnivorous ghost bats shelter within caves, and the rabbit-eared bilby and the small marsupial mulgara scamper along the valley floors. Some species of dragonflies are found only in these gorges and the diverse reptilian fauna that feeds on insects and small invertebrates includes endemic geckoes, skinks, legless lizards and blind snakes. Even fruit-and-nectar-feeding black flying foxes have a large camp in the oasis-like Millstream-Chichester National Park, making it the southernmost flying fox colony in the west.

Silhouetted by the setting sun, a male wallaroo becomes an outline of solid muscle, ready for fight or flight.

Beyond the Horizon: Western Australia

Starkly sculptural against the dusky sky, boabs grow near rivers or creeks and discard their leaves to reduce evaporation during times of drought.

The ancient geological heritage of the Pilbara has bequeathed the region a rich legacy of minerals, oil and gases. Iron ore mined from iron formations in the Hamersley Ranges produces the most significant yields, followed by oil, condensate and natural gas. Iron ore is the product of chemical sedimentation that formed the characteristically red rocks over 2.5 million years to a thickness of more than 2 km (1¼ miles). The accessibility of these ore-rich rocks makes it comparatively easy to extract them via open-pit mining for export overseas. Off the Pilbara coast, the Carnarvon Basin is the region's largest repository of oil and natural gas, the state's largest export industries. Over 77 per cent of Western Australia's gas is mined here and a proportion is piped directly to the domestic market via endless kilometres of pipelines.

However challenging the hot and dry environment of the Pilbara is to humans, the ranges and the Great Sandy Desert into which they merge are by no means devoid of life. Bright yellow and green budgerigars and little corellas belonging to the cockatoo family arrive in large raucous flocks to feed on the grasses of the semi-arid grasslands and woodlands, and bring bright flecks of colour to the dry landscape. Both bird species are widespread throughout the drier parts of the country, and little corellas have also adapted to urban coastal areas. The yellow/green variety of budgie is the original, true form of this bird from which the popular pet stocks originated. In the wild, frenetic budgie flocks are occasionally joined by escapee domestic-bred individuals that stand out in fashionable shades of blue, lilac, pure yellow, white or grey. Compared with these highly mobile flock birds, the large, flightless emus that frequent the region have a slower-paced lifestyle and may live in groups or alone, feeding on a varied diet of fruits, leaves and insects. Emus, Australia's bird emblem, have lost the feather structure necessary for flying and instead have a coat of drooping, double-shafted feathers that give the birds the appearance of gigantic, sooty feather dusters. Despite their considerable height of up to 2 m (6½ ft), emus can be surprisingly quick on their feet if necessary and use their long scaly legs to cover much ground in a short period of time.

remote riches

The northernmost section of Western Australia is an area best placed at the extreme end of any spectrum of description: in age, rugged beauty, remoteness and richness of plant and animal species, the Kimberley is a benchmark for many other regions on this ancient continent. Extending east and north-east from the coastal pearling town of Broome and the Dampier Peninsula, the Kimberley is separated from the Pilbara by the western reaches of the Great Sandy Desert, that extends from the blue waters of the Indian Ocean all the way to the centre of the continent. The barrenness and searing heat of this desert belies its distant history as a vast inland ocean whose sands and silts were washed down from the once massive Kimberley mountains and left in sediments up to 6 km (3¾ miles) deep. Sedimentation and the trapping of organic plant material from ancient forests around 250 million years ago, followed by intermittent lava intrusions into the rocky Kimberley around 100 million years later, were ultimately responsible for the cache of coal, gas, oil and the large diamond deposits that now comprise the geological riches of the area.

The Kimberley has a rich Aboriginal history spanning at least 40,000 years and Aboriginal communities occupy significant areas of land, particularly along the tropical coast. The indigenous way of life, especially among those living in the coastal areas such as the Yawuru people of Roebuck Bay, is founded on the bounty of the ocean and the tidal mudflats that provide a rich and variable menu. Fish like threadfin salmon, bluebone and barramundi, dugong, stingrays, shellfish such as pipis, oysters, cockles and clams, and mudcrabs and marine turtles and their eggs provide a protein-rich diet, and pearl shells provide a traditional object of trade with other tribes. With the arrival of white settlers, the abundance of the north-west giant pearl oyster in the waters off Broome became at once an asset and a liability for local Aborigines. Attempts to settle the area for pastoralism in the 1860s were accompanied by violent clashes between settlers and Aborigines competing for precious parcels of land. When this venture failed, pearling became a major industry later that century, drawing in large numbers of Japanese, Chinese, Malay and European pearl fishers to the area. Pearling is a smaller industry today, but Aboriginal people still struggle to maintain a fading lifestyle that is now under intense pressure from the invasion of ever-increasing tourism.

Throughout the Kimberley, images of the region's long Aboriginal heritage are captured in the rock art that consists of delicate pastel drawings on rock surfaces and cave walls. Made using chalks, earth and ochres, the paintings tell remarkable stories of the local people, cultures and events. The most intriguing of these, the Gwion Gwion paintings of the Drysdale River, are estimated to be more than 17,000 years old and were dated with the help of a fossilised wasp nest that covered part of a painting. Gwion paintings are often wrongly referred to as 'Bradshaw' paintings after the first European who reported them to the Western world in 1891. The paintings depict human figures, some with long

Notably devoid of plant life, the interior of this gorge provides an intense experience of water inexorably and urgently rushing past walls of strikingly layered sediment.

▶ The cascading waters rushing down along the layered walls of Hancock Gorge culminate in a still pool at its base. The gorge country of Karijini National Park is as spectacular as it is rugged and provides evidence of the water's power to sculpt the landscape given sufficient time.

◀ Kalbarri National Park, storm at Red Bluff. Though spectacular and rugged, the West Australian coast is treacherous and proved fatal to many early Dutch explorers whose ships ran aground with little chance of rescue.

ponytails, some apparently dancing or floating, and with facial profiles featuring aquiline noses that do not appear in more recent Aboriginal art. The equally well-known but more recent Wandjina paintings by comparison appear more stylised and are of large-eyed, mouthless figures with ornate head adornments that are thought to be the shadows of ancestors. The paintings are maintained and retouched regularly as part of the ongoing culture of local Aboriginal groups.

Aboriginal people and 'country' are fundamental elements of Australia that are intimately connected and cannot be separated. The land and its first human inhabitants maintain a dynamic relationship in which each informs the other. Kimberley Aborigines are carefully attuned to the heralds of seasonal change and look to the landscape as much as to the behaviour of certain animals for clues. The black kite, a medium-sized bird of prey, is one such herald. The sighting of the distinctively forked tail in the skies of coastal areas such as Roebuck Bay near Broome coincides with the running of ocean trout that are a popular food for locals. The rich pickings of the bay are also appreciated by large aggregations of local and migratory shorebirds (waders). Their significant numbers contributed to affording Roebuck Bay a listing under the international Ramsar convention for the protection and wise use of wetlands. The mudflats, mangroves and grasslands of the Roebuck Plains support up to 100,000 birds and serve as a staging (resting) ground for many domestic and international migrants such as the red-capped plover, bar-tailed godwit, great knot, red-necked stint and curlew sandpiper on their long journeys north and south.

a landscape of wonders

The Kimberley is vast. Pale, sandy floodplains stretch for kilometres and lie dormant during the dry season only to spring to life with the rains of the summer wet season. Vegetation on the plains is sparse and low, with one striking exception — the bulbous boab tree. As in the land of Saint-Exupery's Little Prince, fat boab trees grow across the Kimberley landscape and appeal with whimsical shapes that can resemble slim bottles or round barrels, with a motley assortment of often leafless branches sprouting from the top. The fibrous bark of the boabs makes them difficult to age, but unconfirmed estimates of those with a girth of 9 to 10 m (29–32 ft) reach thousands of years. On a couple of occasions in the 1890s, one or two massive trees hollowed by age were fitted with doors and used as holding gaols by local police. Boabs, like their close African and Madagascan cousins the baobabs, are adapted to dry conditions with widely spread root systems and the ability to drop leaves to reduce evaporation during dry times. Notwithstanding their odd, upside-down appearance, boabs provide a veritable supermarket of useful resources to indigenous people. Bark makes rope and twine, the trees' gum can be used as glue, the trunk holds precious water, and the hard seed pods make multi-purpose household utensils. The boabs' seeds, fruits, leaves and crunchy roots are not only edible but tasty and high in vitamin C, and leaves and fruit have traditional medicinal uses in treating gastric and chest ailments. Given their incredible versatility, it would seem downright reckless to leave home without a store of boab produce when embarking on a desert journey!

The most characteristic features of the Kimberley are its spectacular rock formations sculpted from ancient sandstone deposits and compressed by prehistoric tides. In parts, the landscape softly undulates as sloping hills and flowing plains blend into each other in earthy hues of pinks and ochres. The semi-arid vegetation of spinifex grass and scattered eucalypts thickens only where it flanks one of the river systems that dissect the region. Elsewhere, jagged cliffs erupt out of the alluvial floodplain, creating imposing and impassable walls of rock. Beautiful Windjana Gorge, which cuts through the Napier Range, is flanked by limestone walls that display fossil evidence of the ancient reef from which it was created. Wind, water and time — eons of erosion have created monuments to their creative collaboration.

The beehive formations of Purnululu (Bungle Bungles) in the east Kimberley are the magnificent remnants of a vast quartz sandstone block around 360 million years old that first took shape around 300 million years ago and was further enhanced by the convergence of the Indo-Australian and Pacific plates around 20 million years ago. Its current beehive structure is the result of weathering over the last 20 million years. Purnululu's thin orange and deep moss-green layers of minerals and lichen contribute to an air of sculpted elegance. Despite, or perhaps because of, its monumental age, Purnululu is fragile; climbing of the rock faces is prohibited and the hidden world of gorges and pools is best seen from the air.

The area has great value to the Kija and Jaru people who, as traditional owners, are involved in the management of the park and have cultural responsibility to care for and protect the area. In a traditional sense, 'looking after' Purnululu includes knowing the relevant rituals, beliefs and major cultural sites — trees, rocks and rock pools — of the area, as well as keeping up the performance of ritual cycles. The lifestyle of the Purnululu Aborigines retains elements of a hunter-gatherer culture and makes use of the resources available at different times of the year. In the wet season, fruits, berries, honey and frogs supplement the staples of fish and wildlife, while in the drier times, seeds, roots, nuts and grubs are collected, always ensuring that they are not overharvested or depleted.

Like their African cousins, the baobabs, Australia's quirky-looking boabs are hardy and long-lived. Almost every part of the tree — bark, trunk, fruit, seeds, leaves and roots — has an important use in the life of the Aboriginal people.

In the relentless heat of the Pilbara, hardy eucalypts are well adapted to cope with the harsh climate and the poor soils. Their survival relies on access to groundwater rather than on irregular rainfall.

▲ Yellow spotted monitor, Karijini National Park. These large carnivorous reptiles — one of 26 species of monitor in Australia — can grow to 1.4 m (4.6 ft) in length and forage on carrion as well as other reptiles, frogs and birds' eggs. Their teeth are curved backwards, making chewing impossible, hence prey is usually swallowed whole.

▶ Once widespread across western and central Australia, bilbies are now restricted to the desert areas of Western Australia and the Northern Territory and to a small area of grass country in south-west Queensland. They live in burrows and emerge at night to feed on bulbs, spiders, seeds, termites and other insects. The most serious threats to their survival are predation by foxes and competition from rabbits, both of which are feral pests in Australia.

Freshwater turtles commonly occur in most permanent fresh water across Australia. Where water is temporary, they bury themselves in the muddy ground as the water recedes to wait for the next rains to come.

Sugarloaf Rock, Leeuwin-Naturaliste National Park. This isolated rock in the south-west corner of Western Australia is home to the southernmost breeding colony of the red-tailed tropicbird that is more usually seen in decidedly warmer regions of the Indian and Pacific Oceans.

Limestone pillars in desert sand, Nambung National Park. These strange limestone formations in the middle of a sandy desert are the eroding remains of ancient calcified layers of sand combined with the lime from seashells.

As beautiful as it is bizarre, this small dragon — the thorny devil — is exquisitely suited to life in the desert. As water is a precious resource, tiny capillary grooves along its body guide any rain or dew that settles on its skin directly towards the mouth, ensuring that no moisture is wasted.

Great bowerbird standing inside its bower. Male bowerbirds construct impressive bowers from which to stage their courtship. To adorn his new boudoir, this male has collected shells, rocks and other white debris and displayed them on the ground in front of the bower.

With a wingspan of over 2 m (6½ ft), the majestic wedge-tailed eagle is Australia's largest raptor and widespread across much of the continent. To ensure a prime view of its surroundings, it likes to build its nest in the tallest tree within its territory.

Smartly dressed in a stunningly bright plumage, the Gouldian finch lives in Australia's northern savannas and is dependent on grasses that seed after the wet season. Wildfires can decimate the grasses and threaten the survival of these iconic birds.

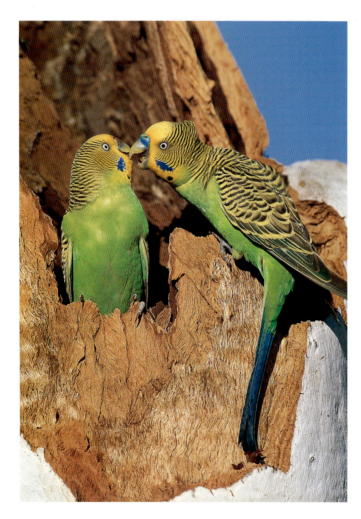

Native to Australia, wild budgerigars are bright green nomadic flock birds that also have yellow and blue markings. Domestic varieties come in a range of colours, and escapees can sometimes be seen as obvious stand-outs in a wild flock.

The peninsula of the François Peron National Park was once a pastoral station and is now part of the spectacular Shark Bay World Heritage Area. Concerted efforts to curb the devastating impacts of feral foxes and cats have enabled the reintroduction of species such as woylies (a small marsupial of the kangaroo family), malleefowl and bilbies in recent years.

On a foundation of granitic rock at Cape Naturaliste National Park flowering coastal heath grows beneath the gnarled remains mallee trees, remnants of a fire that swept through this region years ago.

Daybreak at Kalbarri National Park on the rugged central west coast of Western Australia. The layered cliffs, exposed by wind and wave erosion, rise more than 100 m (328 ft) above the ocean.

Wild Australia

Kakadu & Crocodiles

the 'top end'

It is six a.m. on a clear November morning. The stillness of the night just past still hangs in the paperbark swamps surrounding our boat. As the sun slowly rises, its rays catch on the smallest ripples of water and illuminate low-hanging foliage to a fresh and brilliant green.

Despite the early hour, the temperature has already reached 30°C (86°F) and the air is thickening with early wet season humidity that will envelop everything within a short time. Our boat glides quietly through the water's surface of Yellow Waters lagoon, gently parting water lilies and grasses, avoiding logs and stumps and freshwater turtles and guiding us around the pale and soft-barked melaleuca trees that characterise this wetland landscape. On the tip of an exposed log, a snake-necked darter preens and spreads its wings to dry after an early morning fishing expedition marked a successful start to the day in these rich waters. Some distance along, a jacana negotiates the water surface on impossibly long feet that allow it to move almost weightlessly across the lily pads. The scenery exudes sublime tranquillity, and as the day begins to gain momentum for the swamp's many inhabitants, life seems complete; nothing is missing, nothing in excess.

Of the gamut of national parks encompassing four per cent of Australia, Kakadu National Park is perhaps the most exotic in beauty and diversity. Situated in the tropical 'top end' of the Northern Territory, Kakadu is as famous for its controversial history as it is for the magnificent mosaic of its landscapes and the plethora of life that inhabits each niche.

A range of habitat types are easily distinguishable — the sharp, rocky sandstone escarpments of the vast Arnhem Plateau, shaped by erosion over millions of years; the dense sandstone and coastal monsoon forests; the dry forests, woodlands and creeks of the lowlands; the floodplains and billabongs, and the coastal estuarine areas along the Van Diemen Gulf. Dissected by four rivers with adventurous names such as the Wildman, and the West, South and East Alligator, life in Kakadu revolves around one precious element that is notably absent throughout much of the rest of the continent — water. The seasonality of the 'wet' and the 'dry' (seasons) determines the cycle of life that is utterly dependent on the alternate presence and absence of water for its completion.

Having swapped the boat for the cocooned comfort of an air-conditioned four-wheel drive vehicle and re-emerged an hour later into the spongy humidity of the wet season, the air

Although often photographed in this intimidating defensive posture on or near the ground, the frilled lizard is arboreal and more at home among the canopy or on the trunks of the tropical woodland trees.

Paperbark trees in Jim Jim Creek, Kakadu National Park. Filtered by the early morning fog, sunlight lends an ethereal quality to the swampy landscape. Once the fog dissolves, the day's humidity will become all-encompassing.

is vibrating with the deafening chorus of cicadas while pitch-coloured clouds gather urgently overhead. At times like these, it is impossible not to ponder the hardships of the pioneers who ventured onto this country via land and sea in the early 19th century. Drained by the heat and relentless humidity, exploited by sandflies and mosquitoes, and confronted with unfamiliar and potentially lethal surprises while herding cattle across plains and through creeks and rivers, the European sensibilities of adventurers such as the German Ludwig Leichhardt and the Scot John McDouall Stuart were surely tested to their limits. Leichhardt's determination to find an overland route from Brisbane to the tip of the north saw him lead a party of 10 that set off in 1844 on their way to Port Essington on the Cobourg Peninsula in Arnhem Land. Expecting to 'conduct his party through a grassy and well-watered route' similar to those he had found while exploring the coastal area of Brisbane, Leichhardt was instead confronted with dwindling food supplies, the straying of his cattle (gradually consumed along the trip), and hostile natives who killed one member of his party. Heat stress took its toll on all including his animals to the extent that a bullock carrying the remains of his precious botanical collection (parts of which had been abandoned earlier) plunged itself into a pond for respite and drowned the entire collection. Like Leichhardt, John McDouall Stuart and his party, whose continental crossing from south to north is outlined in the next chapter, endured endless months of deprivations on his attempts to reach the Indian Ocean. His ultimate success in 1862 was an achievement of ground-breaking consequence to all Australian settlers, but the drive to pioneer this route took its toll when Stuart died four years later as a result of the punishment his body had suffered on his journeys. How much easier it is as a modern traveller to appreciate the 'romance' of early pioneerdom in the safe knowledge that relief from the elements is only as far away as the nearest air-conditioned motel.

And yet, the novelty of discovering the sprawling floodplains, the teeming billabongs, ghostly paperbarks and palm-dominated monsoon forests, and the vast assortment of colourful insects, fish, frogs, birds, mammals and reptiles of the north must have been some compensation for the hardship. Kakadu's popularity as a destination in the present time came about only relatively recently. Until Kakadu's gazettal as a national park around the mid 1980s, the top end remained geographically, socially and economically isolated, and its ownership the subject of extensive negotiations between the Australian Government and the Gagadju, its traditional Aboriginal owners. On being declared a national park in 1979 (the third and final stage was declared in 1987), much of the almost 19,800 square kilometres (7645 square miles) of land that uniquely encompass an entire river system were officially returned to the governance of the local Aboriginal people on the agreement that it would subsequently be leased back to the government for management through Parks Australia (formerly the National Parks and Wildlife Service). This arrangement differentiates Kakadu from Arnhem Land, which borders the park to the east and is owned and managed exclusively by Aboriginal people who live in small communities such as Oenpelli, Yirrkala and on Groote Eylandt, and in the bigger townships of Nhulunbuy and Maningrida. Though the landscapes of the two areas are similar, a key difference between the two is the abundance of tourists — while Kakadu has been a popular destination for Australian and international tourists since its gazettal as a national park, Arnhem Land is largely off-limits to whitefellas and tourists and remains a stronghold for Aboriginal people. Traversing Aboriginal country to the few accessible areas such as Oenpelli and the Cobourg Peninsula requires a permit and the maximum number of vehicles allowed to pass through per week is strictly limited to ensure that the Aboriginal values and integrity of the landscape are respected and preserved.

Ignorant of people and politics, the landscapes of Kakadu are vast, ancient and spectacular. Its natural and cultural significance on a global scale saw it included on the World Heritage List in three stages from 1981–1992. Currently, there are 16 Australian natural and cultural icons that have been internationally recognised in this way, including the Kimberley, the Wet Tropics in northern Queensland, the Great Barrier Reef, the Blue Mountains near Sydney and the Riversleigh archaeological digs in Queensland among others.

The name Kakadu comes from the word Gagadju, a local Aboriginal language spoken by the clan group of the same name. The Gagadju and Jawoyn people of the Katherine region are the traditional owners of Kakadu and continue to live within the park. Some are employed as rangers under joint-management arrangements between traditional owners and Parks Australia. Despite its significant status, Kakadu was repeatedly the centre of much controversy in connection with the mining of its uranium resources, most recently in the late 1990s. Uranium was discovered in Kakadu in the mid 1950s and mining of significant deposits commenced within the park's eastern section and in Arnhem Land in the 1970s. While the Ranger Uranium mine continues to operate today, the proposal of a further mine at Jabiluka in 1998 led to extensive protests by the traditional owners, the Mirrar people, and the broader community, and raised the concerns of the United Nations about the potential impact of the proposed mine on the World Heritage values of the area. The decision not to mine was subject to an appeal by the federal government but was upheld, and the proposal abandoned, after ground works had already commenced. Although the mine excavations were back-filled in late 2003, the final resolution for the Mirrar people only came in February 2005 with the signature of an agreement that gave the traditional owners the right to veto any future mining proposals as they have vowed to do.

the 'wet' and the 'dry'

Each year, the colourful stage that is the top end hosts an ancient drama that is played out in two main acts: the wet and the dry. Both are critical to life in Kakadu and alter every aspect of the landscape — its colour, texture, its sounds, and the behaviour of its wild residents. The wet season roughly coincides with the summer months and is heralded by increasing heat and humidity and the gathering of afternoon storm clouds throughout October and November. This time is referred to as the build-up; temperatures rise from a comfortable range in the high 20°Cs (80°Fs) to a less comfortable 35°C (96°F) or more as the humidity climbs to around 90 per cent. Leaving the dry winter months behind, the atmosphere in Kakadu becomes heavy and charged with the promise of the deluge to come; the anticipation of the first rains grows daily. To Aboriginal people, fundamentally in tune with the many signs of seasonal change, the climatic cycle is divided into six distinct periods. The build-up (Gunumeleng) is marked by notable increases in mosquito populations and the dispersal of waterbirds as billabongs are gradually recharged by early rains. The wet season (Gudjuek) from December to March provides a hothouse for thriving plant and animal life as violent thunderstorms unleash rain onto the increasingly saturated land.

The wet unfolds over a period of weeks. Each day, the same scene is played over and over again like the climax of a dramatic opera. Seen from the top of the escarpment, purplish-blue clouds begin to gather in the distance and advance with alarming speed, moving like a solid wall across the alizarin sky and leaving no doubt about their awesome intent. Rolling thunder gains volume as the churning cloud mass approaches, and spectacular lightning bolts explode from the heavens and illuminate the skies. In anticipation of the pending deluge, the landscape grows heavy and quiet. Then the first fat drops fall, and within seconds all is engulfed by the storm, saturated by its warm, life-giving rain. Birds hunker down, rock wallabies seek shelter under rocky outcrops, and flying foxes fold the leathery mantle of their wings tightly around themselves to ride out the torrent. All are at nature's whim.

Once the initial falls have been absorbed and the thirsty ground is sated, the excess water begins to gather as run-off in the escarpment and start its journey through the waterways and onto the plains, recharging what had become barren during the dry. Parched creekbeds absorb the first rush before a steady stream of water gradually fills them and makes its way towards the billabongs, slowly filling each in turn and finally spilling across the plains. Vast expanses of grassland and brown-earth plains disappear beneath the flat veneer of water and life springs from the dormant soil. Sedges, rushes and colourful water lilies emerge as the wet progresses and the wetlands spread over many kilometres, constantly recharged by regular rains.

This is a time of plenty for the waterbirds of Kakadu — as the water soaks into the ground it flushes out frogs, spiders, crickets, grasshoppers and other insects, providing an easy feast for herons, ibis, cormorants and egrets. But this is also a season of extremes. Idyllic scenes of growth and feasting are ruined when prolonged cyclonic rain over the catchments overloads the rivers and vast volumes of water continue to inundate the already submerged plains. A flood has dire consequences for many ground-dwelling animals that find themselves scrambling to safety in trees and on levee banks. Goannas, native rats, marsupial mice such as planigales, snakes and birds, including land rails and swamp hens, seek refuge in the branches of trees, tolerating this uncomfortable arrangement in the hope that the water levels will soon drop. It may take days or weeks before this happens. Ever opportunistic, some predators benefit from the desperation of others; presented with a concentrated menu of tasty options, water pythons swim from refuge to refuge and gorge themselves on the defenceless refugees.

Following months of storms and rain, the dry commences in late April with the retreat of the waters and the promise of respite from heat and humidity. The last stages of the wet (Banggereng) are characterised by violent storms that flatten the speargrass that has thrived during the preceding months. Then the rains ease and the humidity decreases as Yekke takes over in May/June, followed by the late dry season (Wurrgeng/Gurrung) in July/August, when billabongs are once again reduced in size and life congregates around them.

The early dry produces a proliferation of vegetation as the receding water allows seeds to sprout, leaving the floodplains in a mantle of verdant green. Small vertebrates and insects now concentrate in the remaining pools and billabongs, and birds congregate around these rich feeding sites, picking out frogs, tadpoles and small fish while the going is good.

In contrast to the water-dominated environment of the floodplains and billabongs, the forest landscapes of Kakadu that adjoin them — both monsoon and lowland — are less

This beautiful python detects its prey by chemical cues picked up with its flicking toungue or via the heat-senstive pits that are located along its lips.

The luminous pink of the magnificent lotus lily is dramatically offset by its deep green foliage and the darkly reflected sky. The leaves serve as a platform for the comb-crested jacana, a bird whose extremely long toes and light weight allow it to walk on floating plants.

Beneath the tranquil scenery of this lotus-covered wetland, an estuarine crocodile surfaces slowly, barely visible among the vegetation. Crocodiles have nostrils at the tip of their snouts to allow them to stay submerged while breathing.

Uncontrolled wildfires can have a devastating impact on the landscapes of the north. Controlled burns, conducted shortly after the conclusion of the wet season, reduce the natural fuel loads but leave only blackened patches on the paperbark trees.

radically affected by the seasons and are home to suites of wildlife not seen among the wetlands. Pockets of monsoon forest occur close to the coast and in sandstone gorges and are dense ecosystems of fallen logs, rainforest vegetation and Carpentaria palms. The thick canopy allows only occasional streaks of sunlight to penetrate to the moist, litter-covered floor. Its height conveys a sense of a large enclosed space that protects its many colourful inhabitants. Typical of these are characters like the orange-footed scrubfowl, which is also found in North Queensland's tropical rainforests. With its quirky orange legs and oversized feet, the scrubfowl rakes together enormous piles of leaf litter into huge mounds into which it lays a mass of pinkish eggs. A scrubfowl mound may be tended by several birds and can be 3 to 5 m (9¾–16 ft) high and acquire a diameter of up to 12 m (39 ft). However, after investing so much effort in constructing the incubator, the females leave the eggs to their own devices; once the chicks hatch, they have to fend for themselves. The leaf litter of the forest provides habitat for beetles, snails and skinks that are supplemented by a rich yield of seeds, fallen fruit, roots and shoots. Fruits, particularly, sustain the scrubfowl as well as pigeons and fruit-doves such as the strikingly coloured rose-crowned fruit-dove. On the ground, cryptic rainbow pittas hop around foraging for insects and snails which they crack open by bashing their shells against a rock. Small mounds of shattered snail shell are a sure sign that a pitta is likely to be watching from the safety of a shadowy tree trunk nearby.

lowland forests

A more open and uniform vegetation than the monsoon forests distinguishes the lowland forests, which consist predominantly of eucalypts and other myrtaceous plants and an understorey of grasses, herbs and scrub litter. The density of trees decreases as the forest becomes woodland, and the ground beneath features a dense cover of sorghum grasses or spinifex understorey in the hilly areas. This country is the home of many endemic marsupials whose nocturnal lifestyle protects them from the searing heat of the day and allows them to hunt and forage in the cooler calm of night. Top end marsupials come in a variety of shapes and sizes and occupy the entire gamut of niches of forest consumers: from browsers of grasses, shrubs and herbs to foragers of insects and carnivorous predators. A hunter in one instance may become a meal in the next. The largest of the marsupial predators is the carnivorous northern quoll, a cat-like animal weighing up to a kilogram (just over 2 lb) that hunts smaller mammals such as rodents and native rats and mice, reptiles such as skinks and snakes, and large insects, and also supplements its diet with a variety of figs and other fruits.

Equally prominent at the top of the feeding hierarchy is the barking owl, so called because its call resembles that of a small dog, and a number of snakes, including the carpet, children's, olive and black-headed pythons. All prey on smaller mammals including the mouse-like antechinus and planigales, bandicoots and the largely arboreal brush-tailed phascogales that in turn hunt frogs and invertebrates such as spiders and centipedes. These forest environments are also home to over 20 species of insectivorous bats that, though rarely seen, have some of the most fascinating faces of all the top end mammals. Insectivorous bats, or microbats, include a number of now threatened species such as the carnivorous ghost bat, the Arnhem leaf-nosed bat, northern leaf-nosed bat, the Arnhem sheathtail bat and the little north-western freetail bat.

But wildlife activity is not entirely limited to the night. The daytime faces of the Kakadu forests include macropods such as the agile wallaby, the antilopine wallaby and the wallaroo (also known as the euro) that forage on or close to the ground and rely on perennial grasses and shrubs as core components of their diet. A species closely related to the widespread euro, the black wallaroo, is extremely shy and entirely endemic to the rocky escarpment of western and central Arnhem Land.

Predators often encountered during the day include a variety of large monitor lizards or goannas that amble through the scrub, rest along branches or cling to the sides of trees, their slender bodies and sharply clawed feet providing them with a firm grip on any substrate and surprising speed if necessary. At walking pace, the gait of a goanna is slightly awkward as it swings its hips from side to side, its body forming alternating 'S' shapes. Another iconic reptilian character is the frill-necked lizard. Although it is best known for its defensive posture of a large, erect frill, wide-open mouth and aggressive hissing, the frilled lizard is essentially a shy creature that often clings to tree trunks and is so cleverly patterned that it can be difficult to see. The diversity of small mammals and reptiles, and the open terrain of the woodlands, make a sumptuous, easily accessible menu for a variety of raptors including eagles, hawks, falcons, goshawks and kites. While the wedge-tailed eagle is sufficiently large to be a threat to most medium-sized vertebrates, smaller raptors like the crested hawk prefer a diet of tree frogs and stick insects found among foliage. Kites such as the black and whistling kite take some live prey but consume mostly carrion. The square-tailed kite is a specialist among kites and has a penchant for the numerous kinds of honeyeaters that it takes from among the treetops and out of their nests.

Of the many memorable wildlife encounters within Kakadu and other parts of the tropical north, without doubt one of the most impressive is observing a crocodile in its natural territory. Few sights arouse the almost primal state of alertness that results from approaching the edge of a river or inviting billabong to find a prominent slide mark still fresh along the water's edge. On scanning the water surface from a safe distance, a pair of eyes, surprisingly small, can be spotted watching intently. Only the space between the eyes and the tip of the snout, barely visible among the often murky liquid, indicate the size of the reptile carefully guarding its patch. Swimming here is not advisable.

ancient guardians of the waterways

Crocodiles have been branded with a fearsome reputation that detracts from the fascinating aspects of their biology. There are two species — the freshwater and the saltwater crocodile; both can be found in Kadadu and throughout the top end. The smaller freshwater crocodile reaches a maximum length of 2 to 3 m (6½–9¾ ft) and is endemic to Australia, where it inhabits tropical freshwater streams and billabongs and rarely poses a threat to large mammals. The saltwater crocodile is more aptly also called the estuarine crocodile, reflecting the fact that it is mostly estuarine but also able to live in freshwater billabongs, and that it occasionally ventures through the mouth of an estuary into the ocean. The salt tolerance of these crocodiles is due to salt-excreting glands. For a time, the reptiles' habit of making their nests alongside freshwater streams or billabongs led to the speculation that salt glands only developed in adults, but this proved to be incorrect when salt glands were found to be present in small hatchlings.

Little has changed about the biology of crocodiles since the Miocene (23.7–5.3 million years ago), when the first crocodilian remnants appeared in the fossil record. Grown individuals can reach up to 7 m (23 ft) in length and are formidable hunters able to kill any animal game enough to venture too close to the edge of a waterway. Large prey can include buffalo, horses, kangaroos, pigs, dogs and the occasional human and is grabbed by powerful jaws and drowned before being dismembered for easy consumption. However, large kills are opportunistic rather than the norm. A saltwater crocodile's standard diet consists mainly of fish and a variety of crustaceans such as crabs and prawns as well as birds and smaller mammals.

An amusing sight is the milling about of expectant crocodiles underneath a colony of little red flying foxes roosting close to the water's edge at Yellow Waters. Colonies of these fruit bats may comprise several thousand individuals that roost in dense clusters in trees during the day and have the (un)fortunate habit of skimming the water's surface in flight to drink when leaving the roost in the evening. It's a game of Russian roulette for the bats; most make it, others are swiftly snapped up by reptilian jaws chuffed about the home-delivered meal.

The saltwater crocodiles' breeding cycle obeys the seasons of the tropical north. Nesting begins in the early wet season in renewed freshwater swamps, rivers or along a billabong bank that make ideal breeding territories. Using her head, feet and tail, a female constructs a mound from grasses and shrubs cemented with mud and forms a chamber into which she lays between 40 and 60 eggs. Then begins a nervous time for the female. For the next three months or so she guards the nest from a range of predators that may include goannas (monitor lizards), dingoes and pigs keen for a feed of protein-packed crocodile egg. In addition to predators, other dangers lurk. As the wet season progresses, rising water levels may flood the nest and drown the eggs; alternatively, they may fall victim to an early dry season fire if the clutch was laid later in the wet season. Once hatched, small crocodiles are often eaten by larger ones and only a few hatchlings survive to maturity.

While abundant water allows crocodiles to disperse and forage easily during the wet season, the dry season brings with it an adjustment of lifestyle. As the waters retreat and evaporation is high, billabongs shrink and the occupiers can find themselves unwillingly sharing a much reduced patch with several others. Smaller individuals fare worse in this scenario and are often attacked by larger crocodiles crowded into shallow bogs of wet mud. Options are few — sit tight and wait for rain, or venture forth in search of more permanent waters. To avoid the scalding sun, crocodiles may travel at night, but there is no certainty of shelter in the morning as waterholes are scarce and often densely occupied. Toothy skeletons on cracking mud banks serve as tragic reminders of the high price of drought.

But while crocodiles inspire awe, it is the birds of the north that are its most remarkable wildlife. With close to 300 different kinds, the prolific birdlife of the top end accounts for about one-third of all Australian bird species. Northern lowland forests seasonally yield an abundance of nectar from flowering eucalypts and paperbarks and their rich, sweet scent attracts honeyeaters such as red-collared lorikeets, miners and friarbirds. Birds such as the nine exquisite species of native finches living on the Kakadu plains (including the iconic Gouldian finch) are often small and highly dependent on seeding grasses. Although the dry is usually a time of plenty, the transition from dry season to wet marks a time of austerity for these birds. The quality of the previous season's rainfall and the extent of fires within the landscape critically affect the availability of seeds of wet season staples like

After a monsoonal downpour, a red-collared lorikeet licks up the precious moisture from the trunk of a eucalypt.

Merten's water monitor in a creek, Litchfield National Park. This lovely olive-coloured dragon reaches around a metre (39 in) in size and divides its time between a life in the trees and in the water. It forages under water and along creek edges for crabs, fish and frogs, and can stay submerged for long periods.

Kakadu & Crocodiles: the 'top end'

cockatoo grass and soft spinifex. The amount of these seeds available to Gouldians in turn affects breeding success and survival of juvenile and adult birds.

the role of fire

The peak of the dry season brings a potentially serious and often underestimated threat to the delicate woodland communities — fire. Although fires are not uncommon and to some degree necessary for the regeneration of grasslands and woodlands, it's the timing and frequency of the fire that determines the difference between renewal or devastation. Early in the dry, with the landscape still green from the post-wet flourish, a fire will stay low to the ground, feeding on old woody debris and browning blades of grass with little impact on tree canopies. This is not the case in the later part of the season. As the last rains become a distant memory, the flushes of new foliage, thickets of tall grasses, and the abundant yield of nectar dwindles, increasing the survival pressure on all species that depend on them. By now, much of the landscape is completely dry. To avoid excessive evaporation, lowland trees and shrubs discard much of their foliage at this time of the season as the dense cover of storm-flattened grasses becomes tinder-dry. The ground is littered with highly flammable debris and water is now at a premium — waterholes have shrunk or dried up entirely and the flow of creeks is much reduced. This is the time when seed eaters such as finches look for shed sorghum blades to construct their globe-shaped nests for breeding. A fire at this late stage of the dry season can have a devastating effect as all layers of the forest and woodland — ground, shrubs and trees are vulnerable.

Whether ignited by lightning or through human intervention, the fast-moving flames consume everything in their way. The wildlife most immediately affected are the ground-dwellers — kangaroos, smaller marsupials, snakes, lizards, frogs and insects — that struggle to escape the inferno by staying ahead of its front. Many don't make it, either because they are slow movers or because the speed of the fire catches them by surprise. But even for those whose lives are spared, the impact on their habitats is profound. Shelter previously provided by stands of tall grasses, leaf litter, fallen logs and hollow tree trunks is obliterated, along with almost all remaining food resources. The toll on insects and small snakes and skinks is vast, leaving the menu of insect-eaters and small carnivores drastically depleted. Grass seeds have been lost along with the grasses that produced them, and flocks of finches are left to seek food beyond the boundaries of the fire. Woodland trees, to some extent adapted to fire, have lost all foliage, leaving little or no shelter for birds or arboreal marsupials. It may be weeks or even months before the rains are due and any regeneration of the scarred landscape is possible.

Reference to the impact of wildfire on Australia's ecosystems forms part of the introduction to this book in the context of Australia's geological evolution. It is thought that as early as the Miocene epoch (23.7–5.3 million years ago), increasingly arid conditions provided the basis for fire events which eventually, around 130,000 years ago, became sufficiently frequent to cause plants to develop a degree of fire tolerance to survive. These were conditions under which eucalypts and other myrtaceous plants and proteoids (a family of hardy flowering plants that includes South Africa's proteas) were favoured, and their tolerance to a degree of exposure to fire has allowed them to persist over time. The use of fire as a landscape-management tool by Aboriginal people, however, and the lack of such management regimes by modern Australians continue to be a source of much debate.

Although Aboriginal people were once entirely nomadic and lived by an ethic of 'looking after country', the lighting of fires in savanna and woodland country has been a part of indigenous culture for tens of thousands of years. There were many reasons for lighting fires, ranging from improving navigability to communicating the presence of a mob, to flushing out wildlife for hunting and consumption and burning off dead vegetation to stimulate regrowth and provide new habitat for favoured wildlife species. The critical factors of traditional burning are the scale and timing of a burn. Aware of the risks associated with burning land late in the dry season (as outlined earlier), Aboriginal 'cool' burns were traditionally conducted in the earlier part of the dry. This minimised the likelihood of the escalation of the fire and ensured the maximum potential for regeneration before the extreme conditions of the late dry. Another important factor in traditional burning regimes was that burns were usually conducted in patches bordered by natural fire barriers, allowing the recolonisation of each burnt patch by wildlife sheltering in surrounding unburnt patches. In this way, the landscape was divided into a mosaic of burnt and unburnt areas, and once a patch had been burnt, no further burn would be conducted until it had fully regenerated.

Until recently, modern land managers failed to recognise the benefits of these traditional burning practices in containing natural fuel loads over time. The failure to implement considered burning regimes led to the build-up of large quantities of flammable debris which ultimately fuelled searing, uncontrollable wildfires that obliterated the landscape and its inhabitants. The combined impacts of fires that are too hot and too frequent are the loss of plant species and wildlife habitat from burnt sites that may cover hundreds or even thousands of hectares. Once the native plant composition has been seriously compromised, exotic plants and feral animals may increase in abundance to fill the niche and new management issues arise. Gamba grass, an exotic grass imported from West Africa and cultivated as stock feed, has spread through the northern landscape and reached pest status as a result of the demise of native grasses largely due to fire. Concerted efforts are now underway in northern and central Australia to reinstate traditional Aboriginal burning regimes and to increase the involvement of Aboriginal people in managing the land more sustainably. Managing the impact of fire is a critical component of caring for the Australian savanna country of Kakadu and beyond.

For all their remarkable beauty, the landscapes of Kakadu face a number of insidious threats less obviously devastating than fire but with as much potential to damage the balance of life. Despite its seeming isolation from the densely settled southern coastal regions, the top end has been equally affected by the introduction of domestic animals, exotic (non-native) plants and other foreign species that have proliferated and thrived. Horses, cattle, pigs, cats and buffalo are all found in the park, although large culling efforts in the 1980s successfully reduced the vast numbers of buffalo that had bred up over decades.

Wild buffalo herds, initially introduced by early British settlers, leave a physical mark on fragile wetland ecosystems by their sheer weight and size which results in the creation of deep tracks in moist ground. While moving between estuarine streams and freshwater billabongs during the drier parts of the year, the channels created by buffalo lead to the intrusion of brackish salt water that contaminates the billabong and alienates or kills the freshwater-dependent species. Given the reliance on and concentration of wildlife around the scarce freshwater pools in the dry season, the contamination of a billabong impacts broadly on bird and mammal communities and in turn further increases the pressure on remaining freshwater sources. Buffalo numbers in Kakadu continue to be actively managed by rangers but eradication is unlikely.

Throughout Kakadu and the top end, feral cats have found the diverse menu of small native rats, mice, frogs, skinks and birds particularly accommodating, and many years of predation have had serious impacts on the populations of these animals. Although often caught and eaten by Aboriginal people in the central arid regions of Australia, cats are not high on the menu in the top end. Cat numbers are almost impossible to control and neither trapping, shooting nor any other methods of cat control have so far managed to effectively curb their numbers. Wherever individuals remain, reinvasion of areas with reduced cat numbers is only a matter of time.

The most recent newcomer to Kakadu's foreign fauna is neither heavy on the landscape nor a predator of native species but a highly adaptable amphibian. Long anticipated on its steady westward journey, the cane toad first arrived in the park in 2001 and quickly made itself at home around its freshwater habitats. Unfamiliar with this poisonous amphibian, the toad has proved a deadly surprise to many of Kakadu's predators. In its wake, this South American native has left the corpses of crocodiles, snakes, goannas and the northern quoll, whose populations had already declined from competition with cats. Rapid efforts to save the quoll have included the relocation of populations to offshore islands that are now being carefully monitored for possible toad invasions. Although it is possible to reduce toad populations locally through strategic trapping during the dry season, there are currently no effective means of permanently controlling or eradicating them. Considerable investment continues to be made in efforts to curb their continued invasion of new areas such as the Western Australian Kimberley region, where their impact on delicate native fauna is likely to be devastating.

Often no more than a trickle during the driest parts of the year, Tolmer Falls in Litchfield National Park have become a pounding mass of water as a result of the wet season rains.

The tall, willowy brolga is one of two Australian cranes. During the mating season in November/December, pairs of brolgas perform theatrical mating dances on the wetland plains. Focused entirely on each other, the dances involve bowing, leaping and open-wing displays accompanied by loud trumpeting calls.

One of five species of white egrets found in Australia, the cattle egret owes its name to its habit of feeding on pastureland among cows and other grazers. During the breeding season, its plumage changes from regal snow white to bright orange and rusty-brown along the head, chest and back.

Billabongs such as this one are waterholes created when rivers or creeks flow during a flood and are isolated once the flood subsides. The origin of the word 'billabong' is the subject of some debate but is commonly interpreted to mean 'waterhole' in Aboriginal language.

Kakadu & Crocodiles: the 'top end'

At the end of a long day's foraging for seed among woodland and shrubland, a flock of little corellas quenches its thirst along the edge of the Mary River.

▶ The barking owl is moderately common in forests and woodlands of northern, eastern and south-west Australia and owes its name to its dog-like double bark call. While it feeds on insects through most of the year, a need for more protein during the breeding season sees it hunt for small gliders and even rabbits.

◀ At the height of the monsoon, rivers and creeks break their banks and inundate the landscape. Once the waters recede, their highest levels will be marked by debris caught in tree branches and along the trunks of the pandanus palms.

Wild Australia

Neck outstretched in watchful alertness, the pied heron is on the lookout for its next meal. While fish and frogs are central to its menu, it has adapted well to human landscapes and can often be found scavenging among rubbish tips.

Towards the end of the dry season, many waterholes dry up and disappear. Huge flocks of wandering whistling ducks are among the plethora of waterbirds that congregate around the remaining water sources, such as here at the Yellow Water lagoon.

Paperbarks are quintessential wetland trees; at least 10 species of paperbark can be found in Kakadu. During the dry season, the ground beneath them may dry out and become covered in grass. In the wet, the swamps and floodplains become inundated with water and aquatic life abounds as land-dwelling wildlife moves to drier ground.

At the peak of the wet season this crocodile has plenty of cool mud to wallow in without encroaching on its neighbours. As the wet season wanes, waterholes dry up and crocodiles are forced to share their patch with many others or move on in search of moisture elsewhere.

After hours of the oppressive heat and humidity that accompany the rumbling build-up of clouds, a wet season storm unleashes its awesome energy onto the Kakadu landscape. Bolts of white lightning tear open the sky as deafening thunderclaps obscure all other sounds.

With one eye directed at the darkening sky, a blue-winged kookaburra is settling for the night. The blue-winged kookaburra lacks the raucous call of the famed laughing kookaburras of eastern Australia, producing instead a short cackling sound.

Wild Australia

Blue Sky, Red Earth

red centre

Sandy, barren, hot: used to describe so many desert landscapes, these terms are utterly inadequate to impart the vast and ancient heart that pulses in the centre of Australia.

Far removed from any coastline and 'outback' of anything deemed habitable by the earliest Europeans, the red centre defies description with predictable clichés. Instead it demands a far more imaginative vocabulary that is able to evoke the shapes of its remarkably sculpted rocks, the boldly rich yet soft colours, the silky/rough liquid textures that gently blend and starkly contrast, and the feel of subtly scented desert breeze, dry, brittle, and parching during summer. Recollections of the centre rarely leave out words like vibrant, vast and mystical, invariably tempered with more confronting qualifiers such as desolate and unforgiving. Words such as these comprise a basic paintbox to describe not just the appearance of the land, but also the emotions and instinctive responses to landscape features whose creation predates human comprehension. Befitting of their age and history, the landscapes of central Australia make a statement of pared-down simplicity: no clutter and plenty of space.

The region known as central Australia is not marked as such on any map but refers to an area that includes roughly the southern half of the Northern Territory as well as sections of Western Australia, South Australia, Queensland and New South Wales. Its actual extent depends on where the imaginary boundary line is drawn; at its most compact, it encompasses around 300,000 square km (115,830 square miles) that fan out from the central hub of Alice Springs. Encompassed within this vast space are mountain ranges, outcrops and escarpments, isolated mesas, endless plains of stone and sand, and lakes consisting of clay, salt and occasionally water. As in the tropical north, life in the red centre ebbs and swells with the rains whose infrequent arrival can culminate in surging torrents, brimming lakes and cascading watermasses, and whose long absences can deprive the ground of even the last drop of moisture, leaving only cracked clay or a thin crust of white salt to mark the space it abandoned. And infrequent they are — the long distances to the sea and the lack of moisture in the air make cloud-cover a rare event; relentless blue skies and a searing sun meanwhile guarantee the high evaporation rates that complete the arid climate. Throughout the central regions, rains may range

The steep, sharp-edged red rock walls of Redbank Gorge shelter one of a number of permanent water bodies that occur throughout the West MacDonnell Ranges and support life in the arid red centre.

Large and slow-moving, blue-tongue skinks live on sandy plains and among dunes and stony hills and have a variable diet of flowers, fruits and foliage as well as small vertebrates, snails and eggs. The alarmingly blue tongue is used to threaten potential predators.

from yearly averages of 125 mm to 300 mm (4¾–11¾ in) and none may fall for years in times of drought. Summer days are characteristically hot but winter climates are cool and even cold. Night-time temperatures range from 40°C (104°F) to around 20°C (68°F) in the summer, and from the high teens to a chilly 0°C (32°F) or so on winter nights.

plant adaptations

The vegetation of the outback has adapted to the moisture-depleting conditions with some basic structural modifications. For the most part, broad and lush-green foliage is out, and smallish pale waxy leaves or thin water-retaining branchlets are in. A further common characteristic is foliage that hangs or droops, effectively minimising the leaf surface exposed to the sun. In general, plants have adapted either by developing resilience to exposure or by confining themselves to particular habitat niches such as floodplains or sheltered gorges. The plants of the plains are mostly low-growing and hardy and many have a short life cycle that requires only brief periods of moisture to trigger a rapid cycle of germination, flowering, fertilisation and seed production. These 'ephemerals' include grasses, pea flowers, the succulent pink, purple and white parakeelyas, the fluffy brush-like mulla mullas and some of the many types of daisies that carpet the watered plains in shades of yellow, white, pink and blue after rain. Perennial, non-dying plant groups grow where soil moisture remains higher throughout the year and include emu bushes, native hibiscuses and yellow-flowering cassia shrubs that tolerate a variety of soils and can cope with a substrate of sand and rocks. Shorter periods of drought cause some perennials to drop their leaves to survive but extended drought will kill them. Paperbarks, grevilleas and hakeas also contribute to the scrubby flora, minimising evaporation with very small or needle-like leaves and producing showy, nectar-filled flowers that provide a core food source for nectar-feeding birds and insects.

Among the taller tree species, river red gums, ghost gums and bloodwoods dominate and occur mostly as individual trees or small stands. Small woodlands of coolabahs are the closest ecosystems to the forests of the distant coasts and, except for the hardy multi-stemmed mallees, exist only on or near creek banks and floodplains where groundwater persists throughout the year. Much hardier by comparison are the desert oaks that grow on sandy plains and dunes far removed from any apparent water. Apart from dark-green slender branchlets beset with tiny tooth-like leaves that minimise evaporation, the desert oak has an ingeniously conservative growth strategy. Its seedlings develop a straight, branchless trunk to a height of several metres and then cease any further visible growth above ground until its roots have tapped into the water table many metres below. This may take years, and the skinny upright trunk and shaggy drooping branchlets in the meantime give the young oaks the quirky appearance of the faceless hairy character from the sixties TV comedy *The Adams Family*.

The most typical and widespread group of shrubs and trees of the centre, however, are the wattles of the Acacia family. Wherever you are in the centre, a hardy wattle is never far away, and despite the many different kinds of wattles, an abundance of small spherical yellow flowers are one common feature shared by almost all. Wattles with Aboriginal names such as mulga and gidgee grow in a variety of soils from the rocky, gravelly and sandy plains to the heavy clays of the floodplains. And, with the exception of the heavy clays, all of these landscapes are shared with an equally distinctive and adaptable groundcover of great importance to wildlife. Spinifex grass commonly grows in rounded mounds or hummocks and each plant forms a small prickly island separate from its nearest neighbours. Two attributes give spinifex a role of great importance in the desert ecology. For one, the grassy mounds or rings are important habitat for wildlife such as the small mammals, snakes and other reptiles that shelter among the dense spiky leaves in the heat of the day, and for the budgies, finches and other small birds that feed on the seeds. The dense, compact structure of spinifex and its habit of growing new foliage around the old, dry mounds also make it extremely vulnerable to fire. More than any other desert vegetation, spinifex provides rich fuel for wildfires that allow it to spread through vast areas of the desert.

human survival

For all forms of arid life, adaptation is the key, and one species that is generally poorly adapted and notably sparse in the central arid regions is *Homo sapiens*. Only a very small percentage of Australia's population has proved sufficiently hardy to adjust to the trials of the deserts without the aid of climate-tempering technology. Those that have coped best are the desert Aborigines that have dwelt here for 30,000 years or more, living with the seasons and utilising what the land has to offer to their best advantage. Prior to European arrival, the key survival strategy of the Aborigines was the continuous movement across tribal lands in search of food and water. The locations of vital waterholes, sometimes no more than small hand-dug excavations in the sandy soil, were passed on between generations and the waterholes or soakages carefully maintained over time. The traditional diet of the arid regions was healthy and relatively balanced, high in protein and comparatively low in cholesterol. In the hunter-gatherer tradition, game like emus, kangaroos, wallabies, smaller marsupials and large lizards were hunted to provide ample protein, while tuber roots, fruits and seeds yielded vitamins and fibre and fat witchetty grubs and honey ants made tasty treats.

More than 20 Aboriginal language groups, including the Arrernte and the Pitjantjatjara, lived and moved through central Australia, passing on dreamtime creation stories and other cultural traditions to new generations. As elsewhere, the impact of the first European settlers of the region on indigenous people was profound. Newly arrived pastoralists immediately commandeered traditional food gathering and sacred sites for their cattle, physically displacing Aborigines, banning them from their lands and effectively ending the way of life they had followed for tens of thousands of years. Conflict between traditional and new 'owners' resulted in indiscriminate killings of indigenous people in the 1880s and 1890s before most Aborigines were rounded up into missions and camps away from the new settlements. Efforts to 'assimilate' indigenous people to the European lifestyle began in the 1950s when a number of out-of-town settlements were built to accommodate them and imbue them with a Western way of life. Confinement and the forced assemblage of people from different language groups triggered social and cultural problems and led to a downward spiral for many. Although the relationship between whites and indigenous people gradually improved over time, Aboriginal people were not granted full citizenship rights until the 1960s. Today, many have reached a compromise and live in outstations around Alice Springs and work as artisans or are supported by a government employment programme and look to tourism as the main income of the future. Thanks to the Aboriginal Land Rights Act 1976 much of the less productive land and some pastoral leases have now been returned to the traditional Aboriginal owners, who are learning to manage it as a pastoral business using a combination of traditional and modern land-management practices.

sacred Uluru

One of the most significant pieces of land to be returned to its traditional owners, the Anangu Pitjantjatjara people, in 1985 was Ayers Rock, now referred to by its traditional Pitjantjatjara name of Uluru. To most pragmatic Western visitors, Uluru, though undeniably impressive, is a large slab of red arkose sandstone, the exposed remains of a prehistoric ocean bed turned on its side that is said to continue underground for almost 6 km (3¾ miles). To the Anangu, however, central Australia's most recognisable landmark has a deep cultural significance and is imbued with dreamtime stories that have been passed on for millennia and that are the essence of the local *tjukurpa* or traditional law. To honour the sacred status of the rock, visitors are asked to refrain from climbing the 348 m (1141 ft) to the top and encouraged to walk around its roughly 10-km (6¼-mile) circumference instead. Along the rock, many sacred sites are of particular significance to either men or women and hold stories of Aboriginal mythology that feature totemic animals such as the Mala (rufous hare-wallabies, now extinct on the mainland but the subject of a reintroduction programme) and the serpents Kuniya (woma python) and Liru (various poisonous snakes) whose fabled battle accounts for some rocky features visible today.

From the middle distance, the smooth walls of Uluru dwarf the woody vegetation at its base as it rises massively out of the flat plain. Despite its awesome and dignified proportions, there is a sublime elegance about this huge monolith that has weathered so much change since the first bonding of its sedimentary layers. Change remains an enduring theme for the rock as each day Uluru's exterior is magnificently transformed by the rising and setting sun. In the horizontal light of dawn, the awakening colour of the rock is offset by deeply cast shadows that reveal the many shapes and textures of the rock, including steep gorges, wave-like undulations, and the honey-comb interior of small caves high on the rockface that are home to martins and birds of prey. Every sunrise brings about a gradual morphing of colours of the coarse-grained arkose sandstone: vibrant lilac-blue, pale creamy beige, warm mid-brown, burnt sienna and fiery red are only some of the hues of the red spectrum that clothe the oxidised surface of the rock. Only a few recently flaked patches close to the ground reveal the surprising fact that Uluru's red colour is only skin deep. Its true colour is not red at all but an unremarkable grey, burnished by the reaction of its high iron mineral content with the air.

Of similar cultural significance to the Anangu as Uluru, but multi-domed, taller and coarser in texture, the rounded domes of Kata Tjuta (Pitjantjatjara/Yankuntyatjara for 'many heads') sit along the horizon to the west of Uluru and hail from the same geological era. The sediments that formed both landmarks were deposited around 600 million years ago by sands eroded from ancient mountain ranges and swept into the ocean. Larger pebbles settled first, forming the chunky conglomerate rock of Kata Tjuta, while finer sands were swept out further and resulted in the smooth sandstone of Uluru some 30 km (18 miles) away. While Uluru stands alone in the desert landscape, Kata Tjuta forms an entire landscape of its own. Situated in a desert of spinifex, low shrubs and desert oaks, Kata Tjuta's conglomerate domes are clustered together, separated by steep gorges and rock piles that are the evidence of eons of erosion. Like the great monolith, Kata Tjuta's 36 domes have been smoothed over millions of years by wind and rain and continue to be worn away a little more each year, a constant reminder that the present marks only one instant in the ongoing formation of the planet. The main dome, Mount Olga, has particular spiritual significance

The many colour phases of Uluru are brought about by the angle of the sun reflecting off its mineral sandstone surface. Here, the setting sun catches on the diffusing clouds of a recent rainstorm to drape the sky in soft hues of pink, orange and lilac.

to Anangu men, and like Uluru, parts of Kata Tjuta are off limits to whitefellas out of respect for the spirit ancestors.

In the heart of Australia's red centre, all roads lead to Alice Springs. Endless tracks of sealed and unsealed red sand traverse the deserts and savannas to coasts that are 1500 km (937 miles) away both north and south and further along latitudinal gradients. The absence of man-made structures throughout vast stretches of the landscape sharpens the senses to subtle changes in the scenery. Amid the constant themes of red sand and unending vastness, variety abounds: the presence or absence of hills or dunes and the height and texture of the vegetation can change the character of a landscape within a few short kilometres. Saltbush, spinifex grass and mulga dominate, interspersed by dense yellow-green patches of buffel grass, introduced as pasture and now an invasive environmental weed.

At the centre of the continent, Alice Springs is a convenient yardstick for the surrounding landscape features. On either side of Alice lie the MacDonnell Ranges that stretch for around 300 km (187 miles) to the west and over 100 km (62 miles) to the east. Two main parallel ranges make up these rounded mountains and include the highest peaks west of the Great Dividing Range. The MacDonnell Ranges are surrounded by mulga country, and the eroded debris of the once much taller mountains has created slopes that skirt the cliffs of orange-red quartzite. Unlike the thick eucalypt forest remnants that cover sections of the Great Dividing Range, the ridges of much of the MacDonnells and the parallel Heavitree and Chewings Ranges have a moderate to sparse low tree or shrub cover, leaving rough red rock, vertical cliffs and rolling slopes to strongly define these mountains.

Some of the gorges, chasms, canyons and valleys that bisect the ranges are oases for plant and animal life and also important fire refuge areas where fire-sensitive species as well as relictual species of wetter times exist protected from the harshest elements of the deserts. The polished-white trunks of the ghost gums, deep green cycads and golden-yellow grasses add to a rich and satisfying spectrum of colour. Shaded by the steep gorge walls, the still surface of permanent waterholes reflect the outline of isolated eucalypts that cling to the vertical rock in stubborn defiance of gravity and the unyielding substrate that seems devoid of any life-giving qualities. Only the rich mineral content of the rock itself, dissolved by rain and supplemented by organic detritus, accounts for the survival of these trees.

High up among the rocky slopes, the small and compact shape of a rock wallaby nimbly negotiates the coarse gravel, watched by a circling wedge-tailed eagle whose nest sits on top of a cliff not far away.

cryptic rivers

To the south of the MacDonnells, the hilly sandstone country is smoothly bisected by the Finke River whose winding course adds another feature to the landscapes of the centre. The Finke River is one of the oldest river systems on earth and the elegance of this remarkable watercourse is best appreciated from the loftily elevated perspective of the eagle cruising high above on the lookout for prey on the ground. Far from the expected liquid home to turtles, fish and waterbirds, an elevated view reveals the riverbed to be a pale sandtrack lined with trees but, apart from a series of permanent waterholes in its upper reaches, completely devoid of water. Like all of Australia's inland rivers, the Finke runs briefly only after rain. This leaves its bed to be used as a sandy — and handy — highway through the hilly terrain. On foot, horseback or by car, the Finke serves as an access route to the Finke Gorge National Park and is used as such by all and sundry. Along its dry course, the meandering riverbed yields a few surprises. One such surprise is Palm Valley. In the midst of the dry Aboriginal country of mulga and ironwood woodlands, this narrow sandstone valley reveals a stand of palms that seem as perversely out of place as a cactus on a beach. Tall and tufty, red cabbage palms are usually at home in the coastal forests of Western Australia and New South Wales and this stand is a relict of Australia's Gondwanan heritage when wet and warm climates allowed rainforest to cover most of the continent. The secret of the palms' endurance in the arid conditions of today is a small water supply permanently captured in the porous sandstone hills that feeds the palms via their shallow roots. Once again, water holds the key to life.

Torrential rainfall floods the river system of the Finke only very rarely but when the big rains do come, the results are awesome. Vast volumes of water running off from the surrounding hills pour into the riverbed to form a raging surge that may peak at many metres in height and destroy everything in its path. A flood in early 2000 peaked at close to 10 m (32 ft), which was an astounding 6 m (19½ ft) above the height of the bridge that provides safe passage during lesser rainfalls. The joining of the mostly dry waterholes by the surging river brings about a small miracle in this desert environment: an abundance of fish. Despite its long dry spells, the Finke contains the greatest diversity of fish of any central Australian river basin. Nine species can be found here and are usually contained in rare permanent waterholes such as one found in Glen Helen Gorge. The waterholes are refuges for a diversity of fish like bony bream, Hyrtl's catfish, desert rainbowfish, the Finke mogurnda, Finke hardyhead and the

In the relentless harshness of the arid centre, pockets of vegetation cluster in sheltered gorges and draw in wildlife like this ringneck parrot.

tiny Finke goby that is restricted to the upper reaches of the river. Within just a few days of the rains commencing, the river appears to be brimming with a myriad of small fish that have been flushed out of the waterholes, ready to breed in the brief rush of water.

waterless lakes

The power of rain and its ability to awaken life in the most unlikely places is a recurring theme throughout many of Australia's driest landscapes, and rarely is it more miraculous than in the driest of deserts. Even while it is profoundly absent, the memory of water is fundamentally encrypted in the structure of the landscape it helped to shape. Much of the red centre, including large sections of western Queensland, the south of the Northern Territory and the north-western section of South Australia, are part of one of the largest drainage basins on earth, the Lake Eyre Basin. The basin covers one sixth of Australia and consists largely of gibber (stony) deserts and dunefields, but the occasional presence of water is marked by the many salt-encrusted lakes, playas and claypans that are the temporary repositories of water following rain. Large areas of the Lake Eyre Basin receive only a miserly 150 mm (5¾ in) of rain per year, and years of high rainfall average out at 400 mm (15¾ in) per annum.

The lowest point of the basin is located in its largest saltlake, Lake Eyre, in South Australia, at 15 m (49 ft) below sea level. The size of the Lake Eyre Basin, combined with the infrequent and low rainfalls and extremely high rates of evaporation, mean that rain only very rarely reaches the lake and for a long time after European settlement it was thought to be permanently dry. Although the basin is drained by the large volumes of wet-season water carried by the Georgina and Diamantina Rivers and Cooper Creek that make up western Queensland's Channel Country, these do not usually reach the lake and are swallowed by the desert sands, floodplains and playas on the way. Every now and then, however, sufficiently strong rains in these river systems can fill Lake Eyre within just a few days, sparking a breathtaking explosion of life and a wave of frenzied breeding among wildlife such as frogs, fish, pelicans, herons, egrets, pied stilts and ducks. Estimates of birds during a flood event in 2000/01 ran to between six and eight million birds of around 60 species, and every breeding niche — temporary lignum shrubs, trunks of dead coolabah trees and swampy channel islands — was occupied by breeding adults and their chicks. With each flood, the greatest challenge is that the waters persist until the chicks have fledged and are able to accompany the adults to more permanent feeding grounds. This is not always the case.

quintessential desert country

In the middle of the Lake Eyre Basin, the red sand expanses of the Simpson Desert cover three states including the south-east corner of the Northern Territory, a small south-western section of Queensland and the north-eastern part of South Australia where it borders Sturt's Stony Desert and the Strzelecki Desert to the east. The Simpson consists of the most quintessential 'desert' country south and east of Alice Springs. Hundreds of parallel dunes of fine red sand loosely sprinkled with clumps of sandhill canegrass and low shrubs roll on as far as the eye can see. Some stretch up to 200 km (125 miles) in length and are occasionally offset by patches of red rocks that stabilise the ground to hold small hardy shrubs. Trees are so rare that those that survive here claim the extreme end of the endurance spectrum. Only very few species like the coolabah and three acacias, the rare waddy-wood, the mulga and the gidgee, are tough enough to defy the extreme temperatures and the hot, parching winds that frequently sweep through the desert. Following extensive logging by early settlers, one of the last remaining stands of the tall and rather spindly looking waddy-woods is now designated as a conservation reserve, where the widely spaced trees stand forlornly in a landscape otherwise devoid of sizeable vegetation.

Despite the profound aridity of the Simpson, this sand and gibber desert is home to an amazing variety of wildlife that sensibly has adopted a largely nocturnal lifestyle and is conspicuously absent during the heat of the day. Seemingly desolate red dunes come to life after dark when small desert marsupials emerge from the shelter of logs, shrubs, clumps of grass and burrows to forage, hunt and socialise. Small, sharp-toothed carnivores like the mouse-sized kultarr and the dusky and spinifex hopping-mice hunt for insects and small skinks, and the slightly larger mulgara and ampurta reveal themselves as the creators of delicate but distinctive tracks that pattern the dune sands. An even more cryptic creature, the tiny golden and rarely seen marsupial mole, spends its life entirely underground, 'swimming' through the sand in search of small invertebrates and emerging only rarely, sometimes after rain. A subterranean lifestyle also suits the burrowing desert frogs like Spencer's burrowing frog that spends most of its life beneath the sandy surface, lured into daylight only to feed and breed after the occasional heavy rains.

The small marsupial carnivores of the dunefields disappear by dawn, giving way to the day-shift of birds, reptiles, kangaroos and euros that roam the landscapes of the Simpson and Sturt's Stony Deserts during the day. Many head for the grassy floodplains to forage, but those that appear most comfortable on the dry sandy and rocky substrates are the reptiles. Throughout the deserts, dragons, skinks, geckoes, monitors and snakes abound, adding their distinctive tracks

Playas, saltpans and saltlakes are a common feature of arid central Australia and consist of shallow, salt-encrusted indentations that only fill briefly after rain. These tracks mark the passage of a dingo before the ground had once again dried up to a hard, crusty surface.

◀◀ Strikingly offset by the burnished red of Kata Tjuta, this crow surveys its woodland habitat alongside the ancient rock.

▲ The impressive sight of a wedge-tailed eagle feeding on roadkill is a common one throughout Australia, particularly along the open roads in the centre of the continent.

and scats to the textured desert canvas. Two ornery-looking but well-adapted characters of the plains are the shingle-back lizard and the exquisite and iconic thorny devil. The shingle-back lizard is a large skink with a broad triangular head, short, stumpy legs and tail and rough, shiny scales that cover its entire body and guard well against loss of moisture. Its anti-social habit of throwing back its head and poking out its flat, slate-blue tongue is a defense mechanism designed to deter predators from this slow-moving and therefore vulnerable beast as it ambles about in search of flowers, fruits, invertebrates and smaller skinks. The fantastic thorny devil, by comparison, is at once smaller and more fearsome looking. Although it is only around 10 cm (3¾ in) in length, its Latin name — *Moloch horridus* — is an apt descriptor of the brightly camouflaged, yellowish to reddish brown and black body that is completely covered in sharp-looking spines like those of an old-fashioned rose. On crossing different terrain, the little lizard is able to change its hues to match the colour and texture of the background, allowing it to blend more closely yet. Like the shingle-back, the small devil is a slow and awkward mover and relies on its spines to put off potential predators while it jerkily moves about the landscape in search of the small black ants that make up its sole diet. Its ingenious design allows it to maximise the benefit from any available water: a system of tiny capillary grooves along its body automatically guides any rain or dew that settle on its skin directly towards the mouth to be slowly drunk up. Observing this exquisite and quintessential desert creature move slowly but undeterred across the sand brings on a profound sense of awe at the marvellous partnership of time and chance that produced a creature so perfectly unique.

At the other end of the size spectrum, the largest of the local wildlife, the stocky red kangaroo, occurs throughout much of arid Australia and is active mostly at night and during the cooler parts of the day. It is most at home on the open plains where small groups graze on herbs and grasses and can be found seeking solace from the midday heat under scattered trees. Mature male 'reds' are an impressive sight. At up to 85 kg (187 lb) in weight and 2 m (6½ ft) in height, a large male is a solid block of well-honed muscle that is displayed to its full advantage when he stands upright and alert. Hooded eyelids that protect the eyes against harsh sunlight give the reds a deceptively sleepy look that belies the champion boxer's determination to defend his kin. The 'don't mess with me' muscle tone of a male signals the height of his prowess and is used to defend his females and offspring against other males. Male reds can be formidable fighters and use combat skills practiced in play during childhood and sub-adulthood to defeat competitors by holding them with their forearms and, using the solid tail for balance, pounding the opponent's chest with their powerful hind legs. The thick middle claw on each foot can inflict fatal injuries on an opponent, and it pays to look sufficiently imposing to stave off conflict from the outset. Once wearied by age and no longer victorious, old, scarred males may live out their days alone, away from the stresses of defending a mob of desirable females, and can sometimes be seen roaming the deserts in quiet solitude.

The dunes of the Simpson give way to the vast gibber plains of Sturt's Stony Desert in the north-eastern corner of South Australia. These rocky expanses are the product of thousands of years of wind that carried away the sand and left behind the heavier stones that are known as gibber. The wind-driven abrasion has had the effect of polishing the multi-coloured stones and coating them with a layer of iron oxide, leaving a lustrous sheen known as desert varnish that amplifies the summer heat on the plains. Vegetation here is either absent or consists of isolated clumps of saltbush anchored in the rocky ground, or flushes of ephemeral cover of grasses and herbs after rains. Although water seems unimaginably remote in time and space, this barren desert patch is located on the western edge of the Great Artesian Basin that extends underground over large parts of Queensland, New South Wales and South Australia. This ancient subterranean reservoir of water gives rise to a number of natural springs that are called 'mound springs' for the mound of salt and sand that eventually forms around the seeping and evaporating ponds of water. Suddenly there is life, and although many springs yield only very salty water, others like the Dalhousie Springs are surrounded by paperbarks, saltbush and even date-palms (planted by African cameleers) to form small swampy oases that attract a range of waterbirds.

vast and timeless

One of the most enduring impressions of central Australia is of the unending vastness of its landscapes. For all its subtle changes, its sand and stony gibber plains and gentle undulations, its stubborn vegetation, sandstone ranges, saltlakes and cryptic rivers, the middle of the continent conveys a profound sense of timelessness and space compared with the unceasing sensory stimulation of city life. To some, the relentless blue of the sky and the all-permeating red dust underfoot can become almost claustrophobic, while others find the silence of the plains and the absence of visible civilisation a spiritual experience of peace and a welcome slower pace of life. No one is left unimpressed by the endlessness of the landscape that continues on for hundreds and hundreds of kilometres, traversed since the dawn of man on journeys that take hours, days and many weeks.

The ready connection between the north and south of the continent is made possible by the Stuart Highway that runs through Alice Springs and stands as a reminder of the man who first established this critical link in a monumental feat of determination. During the 1860s, the settlers from various coastal hubs commenced an unspoken race to explore and conquer the unknown depths of the continent and to leave their indelible mark by naming the landscape features along the way. While some individuals paid a high price for their passionate but somewhat naïve curiosity, others went about this endeavour with quiet determination and careful planning.

John McDouall Stuart first set off in 1860 with the intention to establish a route for an overland telegraph line between South Australia and the north that would then be joined to the existing connection from Java to Europe. It is difficult to fathom that his initial team comprised three men, some horses and supplies as they left Stuart Creek to head north into the great unknown. Although carefully prepared, this desert journey and the two subsequent attempts took Stuart and his men to the limits of their endurance. After reaching the Finke River at the edges of the Simpson Desert and following the dry riverbed to the Tanami Desert and to Tennant Creek 450 km (280 miles) north of Alice Springs, Stuart and his men were turned back by attacking Aborigines at well over half way to their destination. Undeterred, Stuart set off again shortly thereafter, but ill health and scurvy took their toll during the many months of the two subsequent trips before the proud but exhausted expedition finally reached the north coast in 1862.

Unlike Stuart's ultimate success, the expedition of his contemporaries James Burke and John Wills to establish an overland route between Victoria and the Gulf of Carpentaria ended in tragedy. Driven by impatience and the ambition to beat Stuart's efforts, the team led by Burke set off from Melbourne in the scorching heat of summer with horses, camels and supplies calculated to last two years. To speed the journey along, Burke decided to abandon some of those supplies along the way and left some of his party at Cooper's Creek in the north of South Australia while he and Wills headed for the Gulf with only limited supplies. A series of infamously tragic events followed when the scurvy-debilitated and chronically exhausted men returned to Cooper's Creek four months later after successfully reaching the Gulf to find the last of their party had departed only hours earlier after giving up any remaining hope of their return. During the subsequent desperate and quickly abandoned attempt to reach a nearby pastoral station, Burke and Wills missed the brief and final return of one of their party to Cooper's Creek and died alone at their camp site in June of 1861.

Today, many years after the hazardous journeys of the early settlers, the red centre appears to retain much of the integrity of its landscapes. Events that occupy our thoughts in modern times occur far away and seem to have little impact on the beat of the red heart of Australia. And yet this old country is not impervious to external influences. Many are already here, blending in subtly to the untrained eye — cats, once pets but now feral, foxes, rabbits, donkeys and camels used by explorers and set free in the desert are only some of the foreigners that are having an indelible impact on the fragile desert. The small native ground-dwelling mammals, birds and reptiles that live here are no match for the stealthy hunting skills of a feral cat or fox, and their numbers have dwindled in the face of sustained predation over decades. The central deserts hold the dubious world record for mammal extinctions — 18 species have been lost since European settlement. Many more are now threatened with imminent extinction. The impact of camels is more insidious. Content in surroundings that resemble those of their native Saudi Arabia, camel numbers have exploded to between 500,000 and one million and are wreaking havoc by polluting and damaging waterholes, destroying the soil crust and causing erosion of the delicate soil, and altering the plant composition by over-browsing the most palatable native plants. In the current era of extinction, the challenges of managing and controlling introduced animals and plants are as vast as the landscapes they occupy. From an ethos of taming this wild country has arisen one of guardianship to protect not just its history but its future.

Like orange flames trapped beneath the ground, the rising sun-illuminated canyon wall reflects in the still water of Ormiston Gorge, MacDonnell Ranges.

As the afternoon sky darkens with the incoming storm, a group of desert oaks grows proudly in the sandy soil. Desert oaks survive where other trees don't, thanks to a root system that grows downwards until it taps into the water table, sometimes taking many years to get there.

Yellow-flowering acacias are widespread and a staple food source for many arid zone nectar-feeders such as the Major Mitchell's (or pink) cockatoo that lives among mallee and mulga scrub.

◀ With its highly distinctive shape, Sturt's desert pea is one of the most striking ephemeral flowers of the arid centre. Its seeds can lie dormant for years until growth conditions become suitable and it completes its entire life cycle in rapid succession, leaving new seeds for the next suitable season.

▶ A fresh pink against the red ground, the parakeelya is a succulent that grows in clumps and copes with the dry conditions by storing moisture in its fleshy leaves.

106 **Blue Sky, Red Earth:** red centre

Rippled red dunes are characteristic of parts of the Simpson Desert. Largely devoid of wildlife during the day, they come alive at night when small marsupial desert-dwellers emerge from their daytime shelters.

The coloured layers of Rainbow Valley's sandstones are the result of water leaching the red iron from the whiter sandstone layers. The dark iron surface layers weather more slowly, while the white sandstone below is more fragile and easily crumbles into piles of white sand.

Many desert frogs spend most of their lives underground and only emerge to feed and breed after heavy rains. Sheltered beneath a creek bed from the dry heat, this Spencer's burrowing frog may not have seen the light of day for many months or even years. When the rains come, it can complete its entire life cycle from tadpole to frog in just 40 days.

At the end of a long day's feeding, a flock of galahs assembles in the dead branches of a eucalypt to preen and settle in for the night.

Blue Sky, Red Earth: red centre

Thanks to good rain in recent weeks, the often dry dunes of the Simpson are dressed in cheerful clusters of flowers.

◂◂ While their tails are short and stumpy, knob-tailed geckoes have unexpectedly long and slender legs. Another anatomical surprise is the long tongue, which comes in handy when cleaning and moisturizing the eyes in the absence of eyelids.

▲ Seemingly out of sheer rock, a lone ghost gum emerges at Ormiston Gorge. Ormiston Creek, which runs through this gorge, is a tributary of the Finke River.

Blue Sky, Red Earth: red centre

The perentie is Australia's largest lizard at up to 2.4 m (7¾ ft) in length. It lives in the arid regions of central and Western Australia and forages for smaller reptiles, frogs, eggs or scavenges on carrion.

Exposed here on the red desert sand, the perentie often seeks shelter from the elements in burrows or deep crevices. While an adult perentie is hard to miss when out and about, its young are extremely shy and very rarely seen.

The many different kinds of acacias or wattles are among the hardiest plants in the desert and come in a large assortment of shapes and sizes, from large trees to dense shrubs.

Wild Australia

In the heart of Australia's arid red centre, plants have adapted to conditions of heat and long periods of drought. Spinifex grasses, wattles and desert oaks grow regardless and are integral aspects of the desert landscape of Uluru-Kata Tjuta National Park.

Blue Sky, Red Earth: red centre

Among the Australian fauna, the dingo is a relative newcomer. Related to an equatorial group of wild dogs, it was introduced by Asian seafarers around 3500–4000 years ago and is thought to have contributed to the extinction of the Tasmanian tiger on the mainland around 3000 years ago.

◀ The small yellow spheres of wattle flowers belong to some of the toughest and most widespread trees and shrubs in Australia. In the desert, they can grow in extremely poor soils and the narrow shape of their waxy leaves helps to minimise evaporation in the hot climate.

▲ The silhouette of a dead tree serves as a reminder of the many different types of plants that have come and gone since the oceanic sediments of Kata Tjuta were deposited around 600 million years ago.

True to its nature as a rock pigeon, the ornately marked spinifex pigeon forages on rocky ground but relies on a source of open water to drink from. It is commonly seen among spinifex grassland, hence its name.

The Devil's Marbles is an odd collection of large, spherical boulders that sits alongside the road between Tennant Creek and Alice Springs. According to Aboriginal legend, they are the eggs of the mythical rainbow serpent.

The Devil's Marbles at sunset.

Blue Sky, Red Earth: red centre

▶ Encountered at close quarters, this wedge-tailed eagle is fixing the photographer with a sharp look of indignation.

▼ Often travelling in large noisy flocks, little corellas bring life to any landscape as they descend *en masse* to feed on the seed of grasses in semi-arid regions to monsoon woodland and shrubland.

Tropical Treasures

Queensland's north

There is something about the very idea of a tropical rainforest that suggests fertility, abundance and constant renewal. From beneath its canopy, a mature rainforest system resembles a giant incubator, a warm, protective, often noisy space that nurtures life in all its forms.

The best way to experience an Australian tropical rainforest such as the Daintree in Far North Queensland is to visit it well rested, with a mind free of distracting thoughts and fully receptive to sensory experiences. Early morning is ideal, as the subtle buzz and hum of small insects precedes the shrill pitch of the cicada chorus that ebbs and swells to drown all other sounds. The temperature is still moderate and the humidity bearable, and underfoot the ground is soft and spongy as the dense layers of litter silently absorb each step. On the ground, inside the decaying remnants of an ancient fallen canopy tree, two centipedes scuttle away as I sink both hands into the rich mahogany-coloured humus and lift it up to inhale its scent. The deep, earthy aroma of rich virgin earth — nothing is more fundamentally grounding than the conscious experience of this junction between death and life.

On a continent as patently dry as Australia, the roughly 2 million hectares (494,000 acres) of remaining rainforest are living reminders of its Gondwanan origins more than 130 million years ago when rainforest covered the entire continent. Around half of these forests can be found in Queensland, where they grow along the ridges and lowlands east of the Great Dividing Range. Tropical rainforests are typically either deciduous or semi-deciduous and differ greatly in plant composition. While upland forests are more uniformly moist and contain life forms such as mosses, tree ferns and slender climbing vines, lowland rainforests generally have more deciduous species and a greater number of layers. They also have more complex life forms, including epiphytic ferns, orchids, fan palms, thick woody vines and large strangler figs. The soils that support rainforest are often shallow, structured soils that are highly fertile but degrade quickly with intensive use. The loamy, porous structure of rainforest soils requires constant topping-up with new decaying leaf matter and other detritus to remain fertile and maintain its role as the foundation of the rainforest ecosystem.

In the wet tropics of northern Queensland, rainforest landscapes blend into each other across a range of altitudes — from the uplands and tablelands over the intermediate eastern escarpment and into the lowland coastal plain. The Atherton Tablelands between Cairns and Innisfail are covered by lush green, undulating country about 800 to 1000 m

These fog-covered piccabeen or bangalow palms are part of the semi-evergreen vine thickets that represent the driest parts of Australia's tropical and subtropical rainforest. Remnant patches of these forests are found from Cape York to inland New South Wales.

Visible from outer space, the magnificent Great Barrier Reef is the biggest structure made by living organisms. Much of it is around two million years old.

(2625–3280 ft) above sea level and feature the region's two highest peaks, Bartle Frere (1657 m/5436 ft) and Bellenden Ker (1591 m/5219 ft). The tablelands make up the northernmost reaches of the volcanic chain that formed the Great Dividing Range, parts of which remained active until less than 5000 years ago. The altitude of the tablelands now serves to temper the tropical climate, while the rich volcanic soils make this ideal rainforest country and the upland home of the iconic southern cassowary and Lumholtz's tree-kangaroo. The remnants of ancient volcanoes that bear evidence to the origins of this area also created the remarkable upland aquatic environment of the Crater Lakes District. The crystal-clear waters of the rainforest-fringed crater lakes of Lake Barrine and Lake Eacham are fed by underground springs that keep the water levels constant and unaffected by drought, and keep the lakes and their surrounds teeming with life. Some, like the Lake Eacham rainbowfish, are endemic to the lakes. The forests of this area offer a richness and diversity of plants that feature over two-thirds of Australia's fern species alone. In addition to a plethora of mammals and reptiles, a massive abundance of birds, bats and butterflies populate the many strata of this thriving rainforest system. Below the tablelands and beyond the escarpment, remnants of coastal lowland rainforest sit on alluvial plains that are occasionally interrupted by the ridges of the Great Dividing Range and smaller mountain chains. Much of the lowlands have been cleared for agriculture and the once vast tracts of tropical rainforest are now concentrated into isolated pockets.

plant diversity of the Wet Tropics

The immense relictual value of Australia's tropical rainforest is best appreciated in the 1200 square km (463 square miles) embraced by the Daintree rainforest in Queensland's far north. One of the most ancient rainforest remnants in the world, only very few other rainforests, among them those of the Amazon, can match its botanical diversity. The Daintree is part of the Wet Tropics World Heritage Area that was declared in 1988 and encompasses 9000 square km (3475 square miles) of coast and hinterland. In sharp contrast to other Australian landscapes, the Wet Tropics are considered remarkably wet even by international standards with rainfall ranging from 1200 to 7600 mm (47–299 in) per year in the wettest parts of the rainforest, although recent years have yielded reduced rain. Plentiful rain and volcanic soils enable the Wet Tropics to support a breathtaking diversity of plant life, and the Daintree hosts 12 of the world's 19 remaining primitive flowering plants. Overall, the Wet Tropics encompass over 3000 plants including palms, ferns, cycads and an amazing profusion of flowering plants; 390 plants are rare or restricted in distribution and 74 are now threatened with extinction. At a time when global change is a daily reality and the future of many living systems is at risk from overdevelopment and climate change, this remarkable diversity is a living repository of information that encodes the past, the present and the future. Many aspects of tropical ecosystems worldwide remain unsolved by science. While most conservationists value the tropics for their natural and cultural significance, more economically convincing arguments for their protection are based around their already substantial importance to the tourism industry and their potential value as a yet insufficiently explored source for medicines. Around 25 per cent of all modern pharmaceuticals currently come from rainforest plants, although less than one per cent of plants have so far been scientifically examined for their possible medicinal value.

Appreciating the plant diversity of Australia's rainforest does not require a degree in botany; an enquiring mind and an unbridled sense of amazement, however, are useful prerequisites. In an environment where so many plants compete for nutrients and pollination and seed-dispersal services, the selective processes of evolution have thoughtfully equipped every plant with exactly the right requirements — however strange — to fill its particular niche. The result is a fantastic collection of oddities that mark the various evolutionary stages of rainforest plants. The primitive flowering plants are an excellent case in point. The copper laurel, or native guava, is a primitive tree that produces smelly flowers and thereby attracts beetles as pollinators. In an effort to avoid self-pollination (a challenge shared by many rainforest species), the copper laurel uses a simple but clever mechanism. To minimise the transfer of pollen to flowers of the same tree, the male and female parts of its flowers are accessible at different times of day. This maximises the chances that beetles that collected pollen while feeding during one part of the day have moved on to another tree at a later stage when the female parts of that tree are accessible and cross-pollination can occur. A different mechanism for avoiding self-pollination is used by the pepper tree, a living member of the Winteraceae, one of the earliest plant families known. Rather than varying the accessibility of different flower parts, the pepper tree is of an even simpler design — it has only male or female flowers on any one tree, making self-pollination impossible. This mechanism is also shared by other rainforest plants such as the introduced avocado that has to be grafted for cultivation as a crop.

The copper laurel's smelly-flower strategy for attracting particular pollinators is also used by *Austrobaileya*, a primitive liane that winds through the canopy and grows up to 15 m (49 ft) in length. Its spiral-shaped flowers have the unexpected perfume of rotting fish that lures only flies as pollinators. Given the considerable demand for the pollination services of native bees and other insects attracted to the plethora of sweet floral scents within a rainforest, producing a stinky odour cleverly utilises the potential of other pollinators with less busy pollination schedules.

The fundamental dependence of rainforest plants on a suite of insects for pollination is readily apparent, but larger animals play an equally important role during the seed-dispersal stage. A good plant strategy for ensuring the wide dispersal of fruits and seeds by a range of wildlife species is to produce portable small fruit and this has been adopted by many rainforest plants. The blue quandong is a tall tree that produces a distinctive blue fruit the shape and size of a small olive. Thanks to its convenient proportions, quandong fruit are eaten by pigeons such as the wompoo fruit-dove as well as by much larger birds such as cassowaries and small mammals like the musky rat-kangaroo. The production of copious amounts of smallish fruit is one factor that explains the success of figs in the tropical rainforest. As well as being compact and nutritious, figs fruit repeatedly and at different times of the year and are a keystone plant group that provides a year-round staple food source for fruit-eaters. And not only do they serve as food, but some figs double as accommodation to tiny specialised fig wasps that bore into the grape-sized fruit and take up residence in its interior, entering and leaving through minute holes in its skin.

Figs are the great adapters of the rainforest in that they have more than one germination strategy. Depending on where seeds land, most figs are able to grow either as free-standing trees that draw nutrients from the ground or as scavengers that grow on other trees, exploiting and eventually killing them. The latter strategy is triggered by birds and tree-dwelling mammals such as flying foxes. Seeds dropped in the forest canopy can land in a hollowed branch or the juncture of branches that forms a vessel for water and detritus to collect and allow the seed to germinate. Figs germinated in this way grow aerial roots downwards along their host tree and eventually — often over many centuries — strangle and destroy the tree that gave them life, leaving the massive, interlaced foundations of their sky-scraping conquerors anchored only in the ground.

Palms and ferns have been a feature of Australian tropical landscapes for over 55 million years and those found today have growth requirements that confine them to specific niches in the forest. The Atherton palm (also known as walking stick palm) is an understorey species endemic to the Atherton Tablelands where the climate is milder than along the tropical coast. Licuala or fan palms by comparison are strictly coastal and cluster together to form entire palm forests that reach over 6 m (19½ ft) in height and produce enormous umbrella-shaped leaves up to 2 m (6½ ft) wide. And while licuala palms prefer freshwater stream banks as substrate, mangrove palms grow only in the soft mud along estuaries and rely on the estuarine tidal waters to carry their seeds away to germinate elsewhere along the bank. The ferns of the tropical rainforest come in all shapes and sizes and are some of the most easily identifiable plants of the ground and mid-canopy layers. Tree ferns are particularly distinctive and can grow many metres tall, raising their fronds into the canopy and leaving only bare trunks at eye-level. The ancient king fern, another relict from a distant pre-dinosaur past, is sometimes confused with a palm due to its colossal size and characteristic of sprouting its huge fronds (up to 5 m/16 ft long) from near-ground level. The absence of a well-developed trunk makes the king fern reliant on thick, rope-like roots to keep it anchored and this structure has served it well for over 300 million years. Less imbued with the dignity of endurance is the stinging tree, one of the less pleasant plant encounters of the rainforest. Stinging trees grow along rainforest edges or in light forest gaps and are benign-looking plants with tall, thin trunks and broad, heart-shaped leaves. Almost invisibly, the trunk and leaves are covered with fine hairs consisting of mineral silica similar to glass. If touched, these hairs embed under the skin and release a painful poison that causes extreme and recurring pain for many months, and there is no effective antidote.

rainforest fauna

The rainforests of Queensland's far north shelter some of Australia's most spectacular fauna that swim, scuttle, slither, walk, run, hop, climb, fly and glide through every conceivable niche. The emerald green and yellow tree snake shares its distinctively bright colouration with the many tree frogs that make up part of its diet. Along a continuum of size, the frogs range from the northern dwarf tree frog's 2 to 3 cm (¾–1¼ in) length to the giant (or white-lipped) tree frog's impressive maximum of just under 14 cm (5½ in). One of the most unique encounters in the Daintree, however, is not with a frog or snake, but with a lizard. Aptly named, Boyd's forest dragon sports rows of large spines along its back and a spiny crest on its head. Long, elegant claws enable the dragon to easily scale the trunk of a tree, and its mottled, bark-like coloration serves to obscure it despite its almost half-metre (20-inch) length. If approached, it edges into the trunk's shadow to remain hidden from view, but in the absence of threat it comes down and feeds on the abundance of crickets, stick insects, cockroaches and spiders found along the floor or lower canopy of the rainforest.

Boyd's forest dragon and many other wildlife species of the Wet Tropics are closely related to New Guinean fauna from which they originated. Most have particular lifestyle requirements that contain their distribution to small areas within Australia. An uncommon but spectacular bird found

Fabulously cryptic, this leaf-tailed gecko with its lichen-like skin mottling is barely visible against the patchy bark of a eucalypt. This tree-dwelling gecko is quite a slow mover, making excellent camouflage a vital asset to survival.

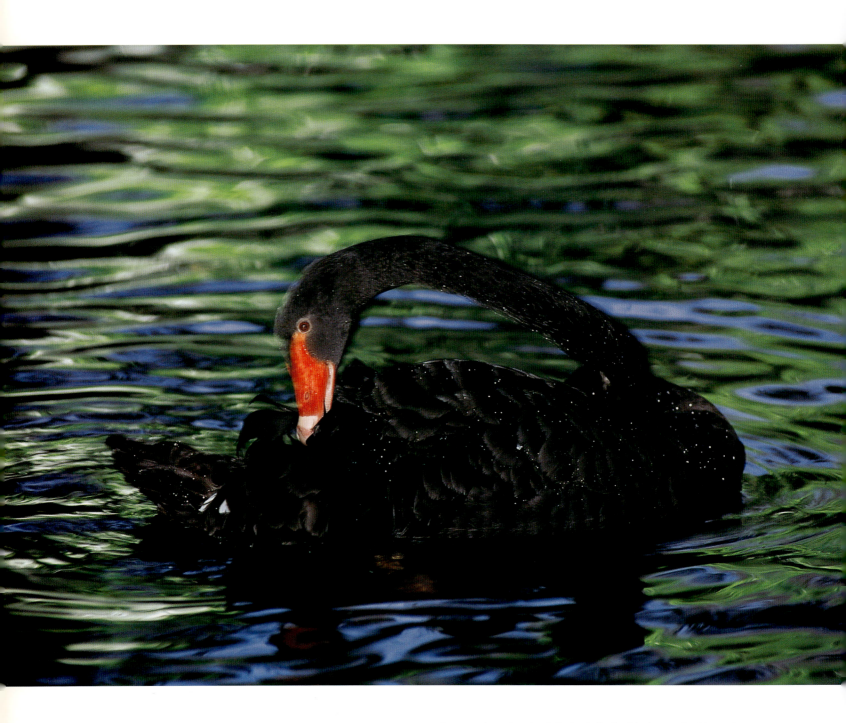

Common in and endemic to Australia, the black swan is at home in large expanses of open water with plentiful vegetation. To arrive at these wetlands, it will travel long distances in large flocks that arrange themselves in long lines. During the moult, however, it is unable to fly at all and must remain in one place until the feathers of its new plumage are fully formed.

in New Guinea and on Cape York's Iron and McIllwraith Ranges is the jewel-coloured eclectus parrot. Both large and vivid in colour, the difference between the male and female eclectus is so marked that they could easily be taken for different species. While the male is an environmentally friendly emerald green with a bright orange bill and red sides, the female is fire-engine red with a black bill and a blue belly and shoulders. The birds' breeding habit of nesting in hollows high up in the canopy makes them reliant on patches of mature forest that may be over 100 years old. Their fate is inextricably linked to this forest; if it were lost, no amount of replanting could provide the habitat needed for these birds to breed.

Equally magnificent and also restricted to northern Cape York is the palm cockatoo. Along with its glossy-black plumage, the palm cockatoo has an upright crest of tall, gently curved feathers, a long, intricately shaped beak that allows it to process palm and pandanus fruit, and bright red, featherless cheeks. As with many parrots, the dexterity with which palm cockatoos use their feet to hold and manoeuvre objects is remarkable and amply compensates for the absence of hands. Far less dexterous by comparison is the large, flightless cassowary that roams the forest floor. Australia is home to two populations of the southern cassowary; the northern population is found on Cape York, the southern in the Wet Tropics. Cassowaries are fruit-eaters that forage on the forest floor and play a critical part in the dispersal of large seeds. After consuming large amounts of forest fruits daily, the birds deposit piles of seed-filled droppings throughout the rainforest and the digestive process is thought to facilitate germination of some plants such as quandongs. Cassowaries stand up to 2 m (6½ ft) tall on stocky, reptilian-looking legs that give them great speed for pursuit or escape when threatened. This substitutes for flight, which has been made impossible by the cassowary's size and a plumage consisting of a mantle of unstructured, drooping black feathers. Despite their renowned ability to defend themselves from predators via aggressive attack, cassowaries are no match for industrious humans or their cars. Southern cassowary numbers have declined rapidly due to the continued clearing and fragmentation of their coastal habitat coveted for development, and many fall victim to traffic while trying to cross roads built through their habitat range. The southern cassowary is now listed as endangered and requires a high degree of active protection to stave off extinction.

remarkable mammals

Not all of the noteworthy rainforest dwellers have feathers. Of the many remarkable mammals of the tropical north, most have arboreal (tree-dwelling) lifestyles and, like their feathered compatriots, highly defined ranges and close relatives in New Guinea. Unfortunately for people, a life high up in the trees makes encounters with tropical mammals extremely rare, and species such as the striped possum and the spotted cuscus and grey cuscus are so rarely seen that they are no more than legendary to those Australians who have heard of them at all. Two appealing northern tree-dwellers belonging to the kangaroo family that enjoy a slightly higher profile are the tree-kangaroos. Rarely seen on the ground, tree-kangaroos resemble their ground-dwelling cousins in overall morphology (body shape) but have a range of specialised adaptations that allow them to live high up in the crowns of rainforest trees and to forage on their abundance of leaves and fruits. Both fore and hindlimbs are broader and have long, curved claws for the grasping and climbing of tree trunks and branches. The tail on the other hand is longer and used as a counter balance while climbing and resting. The entire range of Bennett's tree-kangaroo spans about 70 km (43 miles) from north to south and 50 km (31 miles) from east to west between Cooktown and the Daintree River, and Lumholtz's tree-kangaroo occupies a similarly small range further south. Both species have been affected by the clearing of coastal lowland rainforest and Lumholtz's tree-kangaroo is now found predominantly at higher altitudes in the Atherton Tablelands.

Arguably one of the most charismatic and certainly one of the most controversial of all tropical rainforest dwellers is the spectacled flying fox. This large, colonial fruit bat — one of four species found on the Australian mainland — prefers to roost in tall rainforest and gallery forest but will set up camp in the canopy of other forest types close to their foraging grounds. Spectacled flying foxes are predominantly fruit-eaters and consume at least 35 different rainforest fruits — including figs and lillipillis — which rainforests are able to supply year round. Their nocturnal foraging habit and ability to fly considerable distances gives them a unique role as dispersers of larger seeds within and between rainforest patches. However, the clearing of the bats' preferred foods and their replacement in areas with tropical orchard fruit such as lychees, mangoes and bananas has meant that some dietary adjustments had to be made. To the chagrin of orchardists, spectacled flying foxes seasonally utilise the abundant and easily accessible fruit at orchards and can cause significant crop damage in the process.

Spectacled flying foxes as well as other species of eclectus parrots, palm cockatoos, cassowaries and tree-kangaroos can all be found in New Guinea and serve as living reminders of the connection between the two islands until 14,000–10,000 years ago. Similarities between Australian and New Guinean fauna are largely confined to the tropics, however, and therein lies the greatest threat to their long-term survival — climate change. Tropical soils are rich in nitrogen and nitrogen determines the quality of the vegetation that is the key food source for the wildlife. The increased carbon dioxide levels that are the cause of climate change are reducing the nitrogen in the soils and therefore the nutritional content of the plants. In addition, a mere 1°C (1.8°F) increase in temperature is predicted to decrease the montane rainforest of the Wet Tropics by half, threatening particularly the survival of localised mammals such as the Herbert River ringtail possum, the green possum and Lumholtz's tree-kangaroo. At the time of writing, average global temperatures have risen by 0.7°C (1.3°F) since pre-industrial times and the future of these forests looks grim.

indigenous history

White settlement of the Wet Tropics mirrors that of other iconic Australian areas that were 'discovered' by white man to the detriment of their traditional Aboriginal owners. To the Kuku Yalanji (or Yalariji), the rainforest and the fringing tall open forests and woodlands were once the source of everything they needed to survive — abundant food, shelter and the scene of encounters with other social groups. A number of tribal groups were at home in and around the Daintree for over 9000 years, inhabiting the rainforest itself and the rivers, coastal areas and mountain peaks of the area. The lifestyle of the groups was in tune with the variability of local conditions; housing comprised of thatched huts built near rivers that were easily discarded if weather conditions changed and floods threatened to raise river levels.

Traditional Aboriginal lore is still very much a part of the culture of the tropics and Aboriginal dreamings (traditional tales of how landscape features were created by being 'called' to life) are attached to many of the natural features of the region. A dreaming belonging to the Jirdinji nation of rainforest people that is frequently retold is attached to a natural gorge at Babinda in the southern Atherton Tablelands. The smooth rock formations of the Devil's Pool at the Babinda Boulders are a popular swimming site that is frequented by locals and tourists looking to cool off. However, over the years, swimming at the site has proved lethal for a string of tourists (at least 16) who have met their fate at the Boulders. Intriguingly, the vast majority of those who have died have been men, and there have been no fatalities among local Aborigines. The tale told by the locals is of a young girl Oolana who was promised to, and married, an elder of the local tribe. On the day of their wedding, a wandering tribe happened to pass by and joined in the celebrations. Among them was a handsome young warrior called Dyga, with whom Oolana fell in love and left later that night. When their disappearance was noticed early the next day, both tribes went to look for their respective members and claimed each back. A heartbroken Oolana promptly threw herself into the creek and drowned, causing a great upheaval of rocks and debris at what became the Devil's Pool. The death of young men in modern times is said to be caused by Oolana calling 'wandering men' to her in the mistaken belief that they are Dyga, and young Aborigines are taught early to be wary of the site.

The lives of the Kuku Yalanji people were abruptly threatened when gold was discovered in the Hodgkinson River west of Cairns in 1876. The ensuing goldfever led to violent clashes between Aborigines and white settlers intent on mining the Aboriginal lands unencumbered by respect for Aboriginal sacred sites. The campaign to remove the Aboriginal 'pest' was so thorough that the Kuku Yalanji were (erroneously) thought to have been wiped out by the mid 1890s. The tribal groups of the Wet Tropics were eventually moved to a reserve at the edges of the rainforest in Mossman Gorge north of Cairns during the Second World War where many remain today. More than twenty Aboriginal tribal groups continue to have on-going traditional connections to the Wet Tropics and their immediate surrounds, and each group has customary obligations for the management of their land under Aboriginal law.

immense and intricate

While most of the state is considered semi-arid, approximately two-thirds of coastal Queensland is classified as 'tropical' and much of the remainder as 'subtropical'. From the tip of Cape York Peninsula, the tropical coast extends through the Gulf of Carpentaria and west into the Northern Territory, and south to the Tropic of Capricorn at Rockhampton. Alongside the coast from Cape York to Gladstone lies the Great Barrier Reef that over 2300 km (1437 miles) encompasses over 900 islands and more than 3000 individual coral reefs. Two kinds of reef make up the Reef: fringing reefs that slope off the edges of islands, and true barrier reefs that are found further out at sea. The reefs are formed by small marine polyps that form large colonies and colonial structures. Some excrete lime to generate the solid reef structure onto which other hard and soft corals can attach. Given the deep channel (up to 60 m/196 ft) between the mainland and the outer 'barrier' reef, the conditions necessary for coral growth — warm, clear, salty water with a depth of no more than 30 m (98 ft) to allow the penetration of sunlight — are thought to have come about either through

A green tree snake — in a blue-grey and yellow colour form — devouring a green tree frog in a bright green birdsnest fern.

Tropical Treasures: Queensland's north

Tired from the effort, a female loggerhead returns to the ocean after laying her eggs into a carefully excavated hole on the beach at Mon Repos. Six of the world's seven species of marine turtle can be found in Australian waters; all are now threatened with extinction.

the gradual subsidence of the seabed, allowing coral to keep up its growth rate, or from the gradual rise of the ocean, equally allowing the coral growth to keep pace.

Recognised internationally as a World Heritage Area, the Great Barrier Reef is a dense and intricate web of life that supports living coral, seagrasses, molluscs (clams, snails etc.), echinoderms (sea urchins, sea cucumbers, star fish etc.), crustaceans (prawns, crabs etc.), sponges, worms, and micro-organisms alongside 1500 species of fish, hundreds of birds, and a suite of marine mammals that includes turtles, dugongs, dolphins and whales. The delicate ecosystems of the Great Barrier Reef are vulnerable to a range of threats that include overfishing, and physical damage through storms, shipping operations, pollution and poorly managed tourism. Less immediately apparent but equally serious is the increasing impact of climate change on the coral structures of the reef. The tiny polyps that form the coral can only exist within a narrow temperature band. Water temperatures that fall outside this band by as little as 1–2°C (2–4°F) for more than a few days lead to the demise of these polyps and the death of many species of corals, leaving only the bleached calcareous remains of once thriving and diverse coral colonies. Over time, corals can recover from smaller bleaching events, but repeated periods of unusual temperatures cause permanent damage. Evidence of large-scale coral bleaching provides visible and irrefutable evidence that climate change is a reality, and coral reefs will continue to serve as indicators for temperature rises in the future.

The careful management and protection of the reef is vital to its survival, more than ever in the face of climate change which can only be controlled through significant global reductions in the production of greenhouse gases such as carbon dioxide. Considering the challenges of this goal and the temperature increases predicted irrespective of reduced emissions, increasing the resilience of the reef by maintaining it in a state of health capable of coping with temperature stress is now a primary objective of reef conservation. A milestone in reef conservation in 2004 was the declaration of one-third of the Marine Park as strictly protected, representing a tenfold increase of the area previously under protection. This status affords the reef a reprieve from overfishing, with the government buying back fishing licences from commercial fishing operators. However, the health of coral reefs is now as directly dependent on sustainable pastoral and agricultural practices as on activities that occur in the ocean itself. One of the primary threats to the reef and the living systems of the coastal fringes is pollution, and over 80 per cent of reef pollution originates on the land in the form of sediment, fertilisers and pesticides that are washed from farmlands into rivers and creeks and drain into the Great Barrier Reef's lagoon. This in turn causes algal outbreaks, particularly in the inshore areas, smothering corals and effectively suffocating other life dependent on clear and unpolluted water. The higher abundance of phytoplankton is also thought to play a part in the periodic outbreaks of crown-of-thorns starfish that feed on this minute plant life. While the starfish is naturally a part of the marine ecosystem, large increases in crown-of-thorns cause significant damage to the corals on which they feed.

biological barrier

South of the Wet Tropics, the landscape dramatically changes as it encounters one of the two dry (semi-arid) coastal corridors of the Brigalow Belt. The aridity of this area is due to the absence of coastal ranges that are needed to secure regular rainfall. Low rainfall results in an entirely different, hardier vegetation of open forest and woodland that feature an acacia commonly known as brigalow. Among this drier landscape, only a few high peaks, Mt Elliot, Mt Aberdeen and Mt Abbot, contain unique biodiversity with elements from the Wet Tropics to the north and the Central Mackay Coast rainforests to the south. This northern brigalow corridor, one of two coastal extensions of the Brigalow Belt, represents a major biological barrier to the movement and evolution of tropical species.

The mountains and gorges of Eungella National Park near Mackay have been isolated from other rainforest areas for tens of thousands of years. Eungella's misty mountains of rainforest trees and palms are interspersed with bottlebrushes, river she-oaks and Sydney blue gums that are more typically found in sandy, well-drained soils. Due to its long isolation, Eungella has a distinctive flora and fauna and a number of endemic species. Until recently, it was also home to one of Australia's most unusual amphibians, the gastric brooding frog, which had the remarkable habit of swallowing its eggs and rearing its tadpoles in its stomach. During incubation, the female's stomach secreted a substance that inhibited the production of hydrochloric acid, thereby protecting her brood but also preventing her from eating until she had orally 'given birth' to her brood after about six weeks. The frog's ability to shut off the acid production in its stomach made it the subject of research into the treatment of gastric ulcers and resulted in the development of a new drug. Sadly, the frog disappeared from Eungella in the early 1980s and is now thought extinct.

But the riches of Eungella are plentiful. In addition to two other stream-dwelling frog species found only in this national park, the tall, buttressed Mackay tulip oak, the Eungella honeyeater (a bird) and the orange-sided skink are all unique to this rainforest. Eungella's best-known inhabitant, however, is not restricted to the park but can be found east of the Great Dividing Range from North Queensland to Tasmania and occupies freshwater streams in cool alpine climates as readily

◀ Eclectus parrots live and breed high among the forest canopy. While incubating their eggs, the red and blue females are tended by one or more males that feed both her and her nestlings until they fledge.

▲ A southern cassowary with one of her three chicks in the Atherton Tableland. A force to be reckoned with, a cassowary is highly protective of its young and will aggressively attack any perceived threat, including humans.

as in tropical lowlands. On a continent famed for its unique wildlife, the platypus is in a league of its own. This small (up to 1 kg/2.2 lb in weight) shy, softly furred mammal with webbed feet and an incongruous rubbery bill spends much of the day in the water, using its highly sensitive bill to forage for larvae, small freshwater shrimp and other invertebrates. Out of the water, this solitary mammal lives in simple burrows built into the streambank just above water level and often obscured by clusters of tree roots. Of the three main groups of mammals currently in existence, platypus, along with echidnas, belong to the monotremes, the earliest evolved in evolutionary terms. Without pouches or placentas in which young are able to reach an advanced stage of development, a female platypus lays two eggs which she protects until hatching by curling up in her burrow and folding over her tail to hold the eggs to her belly. After hatching, the female produces milk from ducts on her abdomen on which the young suckle for four to five months, never leaving the burrow. Ancestors of today's platypus lived as early as 15 million years ago and changed little in the last million years. A relictual feature retained by infant platypus is a set of milk teeth similar to the teeth found in their fossil ancestors. These are lost in adulthood, and mature platypus use their tongue and horny grinding plates and ridges in their upper and lower jaws to break down food. Although platypus occur across a long range, their distribution is patchy and their freshwater habitat under considerable pressure. In the absence of sufficient rain, the streams and creeks that are home to platypus and other aquatic life have become primary sources of water for agricultural irrigation. Minimising the alteration and subversion of freshwater streams, and managing water pollution from chemical run-off are vital to ensure the survival of these singularly Australian mammals into the future.

South of the Central Queensland Coast, that includes the Eungella rainforests, lies the second dry corridor of the Brigalow Belt around Rockhampton. This isolates the tropical rainforests of the Central Queensland Coast region from the mainly subtropical rainforests of South East Queensland. Within the semi-arid Brigalow Belt, some of the most diverse and chiefly threatened plant communities are extremely dry forms of rainforest, known as semi-evergreen vine thicket or softwood scrub. These lower and relatively simpler communities contribute significantly to the biodiversity of this region that extends inland from Townsville to Gunnedah in central New South Wales. One of the most distinctive features of many scrubs is the bottle tree (*Brachychiton rupestris*) that grows up to 30 m (98 ft) tall and dwarfs anyone standing next to it. Unfortunately, remnant areas of dry rainforest are prone to invasion by weeds, especially introduced pasture grasses such as buffel, which dramatically increase the risk and intensity of fires that threaten these rainforest systems.

Carnarvon Gorge: a green oasis

Some 400 km (250 miles) to the south-west of Eungella, in the heart of the Brigalow Belt in central Queensland, platypus are among the many wildlife species at home in the spectacular chasms of the Carnarvon Gorge National Park. Towering white sandstone cliffs and brightly coloured layers of sediments deposited over millennia shelter a remnant rainforest enclave of cycads, ferns, Livistona (or cabbage) palms, orchids, fig trees, flowering bottlebrushes and native hibiscus mixed with a few eucalypts. In this otherwise dry inland part of the country, the green 'oasis' of Carnarvon Gorge was created over a period of 200 million years by streams and rivers cutting through sandstone country and slicing chasms up to 600 m (1968 ft) deep into the landscape, leaving tablelands of grassy open forest on either side. A creek flows along the gorge floor and Aboriginal rock art of paintings, stencils and engravings on sandstone overhangs dating back more than 3500 years reveals the significance of this area to local Aboriginals. Sheltered chasms like Carnarvon Gorge are a haven for both humans and wildlife that seek out the creeks and rich vegetation among the cool forest environment. Possums, gliders, owls, lace monitors, echidnas, platypus and a myriad of birds populate the Gorge and fill it with bustling activity at various times of the day and night.

Carnarvon has a function of great importance beyond the boundaries of the gorge. The porous sandstone country of the region absorbs rainwater and acts as an intake aquifer for the Great Artesian Basin, the largest of three underground repositories of fresh water in Australia. The Great Artesian Basin covers almost 1.5 million square km (579,000 square miles) and spreads from the Gulf of Carpentaria in the north to the Darling Downs in Queensland to the south and close to Alice Springs in the west. The Basin is the remains of an ancient inland sea that covered this area from 65–140 million years ago. Dense, waterproof layers of siltstone and shales that formed the seafloor were bedded down over thick layers of sandstone that are now partially exposed along the Great Dividing Range in areas such as Carnarvon. During rain, water slowly seeps through these sandstone layers and is trapped within the basin. When the basin is tapped, the water comes to the surface under its own pressure, providing irrigation water in some of the driest parts of the outback. Nowhere else is Australia's vast age, the complexity of its geology and the resulting interconnectedness of its often distant landscape features as clearly apparent as through the remarkable hydrology of its artesian basins.

This young agile wallaby is feeding on its favourite food — grass. Agile wallabies feed on most types of native grasses and sedges and small groups often aggregate into large mobs at feeding areas.

A popular swimming spot for locals and tourists, the Babinda Boulders in North Queensland's Atherton Tableland are steeped in myth owing to a string of tourist deaths that have occurred there in the past two decades. The deaths are explained by an Aboriginal legend about a young woman calling her lover to her.

The medium-sized eastern water dragon lives along the edges of waterways and has adapted well to an urban lifestyle where cities have encroached on its habitat. During the mating season, male dragons develop reddish-coloured throats and perform territorial head-bobbing displays to defend their section of the creekline.

Where rocky or sandy coastal landscapes and vegetation provide the stage and props of the tropics, the rapidly changing skies of the wet season provide the mood. Rolling slate-grey clouds reflected in the ruffled ocean bring an atmosphere of broodiness; a change from the endless blue skies common at other times of the year.

Tropical Treasures: Queensland's north

The exposed stilt roots of these coastal mangroves at Cape Tribulation enable the trees to take in oxygen from the air as it is scarce in the silted, anaerobic ground beneath.

Sturdy root systems such as the sheet-like buttress roots of this old giant help to balance large trees in the shallow rainforest soil. In addition to improving stability, they also increase the surface area of root able to absorb nutrients that are largely found close to the soil surface.

Tropical Treasures: Queensland's north

Using its specially adapted limbs to grip with, this young Lumholtz tree-kangaroo is scaling a slender tree trunk to seek shelter where it is most at ease — in the canopy.

Wild Australia 147

While captured in amplexus (mating) in this image, the stony-creek frog's mating call is a soft whirring, so quiet as to be almost inaudible to people. True to its name, it lives around streams that have a bed of stones or pebbles.

This elegantly slender tree snake is a joy to behold as it moves quickly and effortlessly among the thin branches of a tree or shrub, parts of its long body and head easily suspended in mid-air. Although it is often called a green tree snake, colours range from black to yellow, olive-green, blue-green or blue across different parts of its range. Frogs, lizards, tadpoles and fish feature prominently on its preferred menu, but it is entirely harmless to humans.

Tropical Treasures: Queensland's north

▶ The platypus is, without doubt, one of the most amazing creatures in Australia. Found along the east and south-east coasts and in Tasmania, this shy mammal lives in freshwater streams, sifting the silty bottom for invertebrates and larvae. Its soft, rubbery bill is equipped with sensitive receptors that help it to find its food among the stirred up silt.

▼ This beautiful frog of the warm and tropical regions of the east tends to live in swamps or ponds surrounded by dense vegetation. Its call sounds remarkably like the plucking of a banjo string, and it is descriptively known as northern banjo frog or scarlet-sided pobblebonk.

◀ The deep chasms of Carnarvon Gorge are over 200 million years old and provide a cool, moist environment for a variety of ferns, cycads, cabbage palms and wildlife that live in this rainforest remnant. Moss-covered walls attest to the constant high levels of moisture in this otherwise dry inland part of Queensland.

Wild Australia

◀ After suffocating its prey with the tightening coils of its muscular body, the amethyst python unhinges its own jaws in order to devour it, slowly inching its upper and lower jaw sections along the body until it is entirely consumed. Larger prey such as a wallaby may take weeks to digest.

▶ The spectacular Boyd's forest dragon is a secretive tropical rainforest resident rarely seen as exposed as in this image. More often than not, it moves into the shadow-side of a tree trunk when approached to avoid being spotted.

Tropical Treasures: Queensland's north

Koala Country

eucalypt forests of the south-east

Across its vast landmass, the Australian continent features a range of landscapes of improbable diversity. In part, this is made possible by the sheer size of the country, which at 7.7 million square km (2.9 million square miles) is equal in size to the mainland United States.

Seen at this relative scale, it's perhaps less surprising that Australia's landscapes include vast coastlines and plunging harbours, a myriad of catchments and river systems, mountain chains, deserts, expansive rangelands, savannas, tropical and subtropical rainforests, dry forests, woodlands and grasslands. Previous chapters have focused on some of the coastal, tropical and desert landscapes of the continent and their natural attributes. Some of the most quintessential Australian plants and animals, however, are at home in and around the eucalypt forests and woodlands of south-eastern Australia that encompass parts of southern Queensland, New South Wales, Victoria and South Australia.

As outlined previously, much of the forest of eastern Australia owes its distribution to good rainfall and rich patches of soil left by volcanic activity. Localised upwellings of lava along the Great Divide from Cape York to central Victoria brought about some obvious landscape markers that remain to this day and include the surprising rock formations of the Glass House Mountains north of Brisbane and the Warrumbungle volcano in northern New South Wales.

Not all volcanic activity resulted in the creation of mountains. In some areas, lava oozing through vents in the earth's crust spread across vast tracts of the land surface, generating and enriching soils that now support temperate rainforests like those on the tablelands of northern New South Wales. Some of the densest eucalypt forests of the eastern coast and hinterland, however, are found in and around the Sydney Basin. This region comprised the southern arm of a freshwater lake about 210 million years ago and its soils originate from richly layered lake sediments of muds and swamp plants that combined with volcanic ash to form soft sandstones and shales. The so-called Hawkesbury sandstones cover around 18,000 square km (7000 square miles) of the Sydney Basin. Most prominently, they shaped the headlands and cliffs of Sydney Harbour and the spectacular multi-layered chasms of the Blue Mountains.

The rugged beauty of the Greater Blue Mountains World Heritage Area stretches across 1 million hectares (2½ million acres) of sandstone escarpment and includes large areas of inaccessible wilderness despite its proximity to Sydney's sprawling suburbia. The rough terrain, sheer cliffs and the density of the vegetation left the Blue Mountains impassable

This red-necked wallaby's pouch is a protective home for its growing occupant. When standing still, the muscular walls of the female's pouch are relaxed to allow it to hang like a soft bag. While moving, the pouch is contracted, gathering the joey tightly to its mother's abdomen.

Remarkable Rocks, Kangaroo Island. Shaped by wind and sea, this odd geological monument perches high on a coastal granite boulder and owes its red-coloured patches to a lichen that grows over parts of it.

Koala Country: eucalypt forests of the south-east

to early explorers until 1813. After years of disappointing attempts to find a passage to better grazing country to the west, an early governor considered that:

' … the idea of extending agriculture beyond the first range of mountains must be given up as the rocks to the west display the most barren and forbidding aspect which men, animals, birds and vegetation have ever been strangers to….' (Governor Philip King, 1758–1808).

As it turned out, this statement held true only for men as 'animals, birds and vegetation' coped just fine with these conditions. The Blue Mountains are quintessential eucalypt country and more than 90 different eucalypt species grow in ecological communities ranging from dry sclerophyll to mallee country to heathlands, wetlands and swamps. Eucalypts are also responsible for the famous bluish haze that often shrouds the valleys and to which the Blue Mountains owe their name. Rays of sunlight strike dust particles and small droplets of moisture and eucalyptus oil that evaporate from the leaves to create the translucent blue tinge.

In 1994 a remarkable chance discovery served as an indicator of the ancient secrets still concealed within the Blue Mountains' impenetrable depths. The Wollemi pine, a tall conifer with a trunk of more than 100 cm (39 in) in thickness and bark that resembles bubbling chocolate, had until then been known only as a fossil dating back to the time of dinosaurs some 90–200 million years ago. After long being consigned to history, a number of these unusual-looking pines were discovered growing on wet rock ledges in a sheltered rainforest canyon. While seedlings have been successfully cultivated since, the location of the original stock is a well-kept secret known only to a handful of people.

iconic plants

Eucalypt trees, including the famous gum trees that feature so prominently in traditional Australian lore, are keystone plants in Australia's native forest systems and first appeared around 35 million years ago. The Myrtaceae family to which the eucalypts belong is an extremely hardy plant family that includes many flowering trees and shrubs that grow in a variety of soils. With their origins in Gondwana, myrtaceous plants are also found in Central and South America and Melanesia. In Australia, bottlebrushes (*Callistemon* spp.), tea trees (*Leptospermum* spp.) and eucalypts are all members of the Myrtaceae, whose distinctive flowers generate plentiful nectar for a plethora of nectar-feeding birds, mammals and insects.

The family also includes the shrubby or slender, medium-sized paperbark (or honey myrtle) trees that grow predominantly in moist, swampy, coastal areas along the coast of the Northern Territory, Cape York and the east coast, as well as in north-western Tasmania and pockets of Western Australia.

Paperbarks (*Melaleuca* spp.) have a distinctive pale bark that flakes off in thin sheets and flower in a great profusion of powder-puff clusters or brushy flowers in shades of red, orange, purple or, most commonly, in creamy whites. The low flammability of the bark has made it a useful cooking aid for Aboriginal people who use it like an oven-bag to wrap food such as fish for cooking in a fire, thereby retaining much of the food's precious moisture. The easily workable and enduring timber of paperbarks was a useful building material for canoes. Paperbarks are of particular importance to wildlife as some may flower in winter and so are a substantial food source when resources are often scarcer than at other times of the year. When in flower, the cloyingly sweet honey-scent of paperbarks attracts noisy flocks of lorikeets, honeyeaters and other local nectar-feeders during the daytime, while flying foxes battle possums and gliders for their nectar bounty at night. Paperbark forests once widely occupied the swampy coastal areas alongside sclerophyll forests, but many of these swamps have been drained for coastal development and farm forestry, leaving some adaptable wildlife to seek out alternative food sources in urban and agricultural areas.

Myrtaceous plants feature prominently in the coastal subtropical and temperate climate ranges, but they are by no means the only trees and shrubs whose flora embellishes these landscapes. Another prominent plant family of Gondwanan ancestry is the Proteaceae. Best known for the stunning African proteas, in Australia they include the distinctive gnarled and stocky banksia shrubs, elegant grevilleas (or spider flowers), waratahs and luminous pin-cushion-flowered hakeas, among others. To allow them to cope with the dry Australian conditions, the striking flowers of the Proteaceae are offset by tough, waxy and narrow leaves that minimise evaporation. While Proteaceae, like Myrtaceae, can be found throughout the country, both thrive in the milder climates of the south east, making the most of the rains and the moderate to fertile soils.

The she-oaks or Casuarinaceae are a family of small, medium-sized to tall trees that feature among south-east forests in rocky, sandy and swampy environments. She-oaks are easily recognisable by their long, drooping branchlets that look more like very thin green stems growing out of slightly wider brown branches. Tiny spikes or 'teeth' along each branchlet constitute the actual leaves which have only a minute surface area that restricts evaporation to a bare minimum. Very small flowers prevent casuarinas from being 'showy' trees or producing much nectar, but their hard brown 'fruits' — really cones that house seeds — are a prized food source for larger species of cockatoos such as the glossy black and red-tailed black cockatoo. She-oaks occur either in separate stands or in association with eucalypts and often flank riparian streams.

Whether as dense sclerophyll forests or sparse woodlands, in deserts or on snow-topped mountains, the 800-odd species of eucalypt that occur across the continent have conquered every climate and developed a dogged resilience to the vagaries of time. There are two main characteristics to which the eucalypts owe their success — tough, drooping leaves that reduce evaporation and a hardy resilience to fire. Different strategies may support the latter. Some eucalypts have lignotubers (woody swellings that are partly or wholly hidden underground) that allow them to survive and reshoot at ground level, while others sprout fresh shoots straight from their charcoaled trunks. The ability to cope with and indeed benefit from wildfires is critical to the eucalypts' success. Many species have tough woody seed capsules that can lie dormant for years and depend on the intense heat of a fire to burst open and release their seeds, thereby providing a third strategy for post-burn regeneration.

the rise of the eucalypts

Despite their prolific distribution throughout most Australian ecosystems, eucalypts have not always dominated the continental forest flora. While already favoured by poor soils, it is possible that the arrival of Aboriginal people years ago contributed to their proliferation. The Aboriginal practice of burning the landscape (outlined in 'Kakadu & Crocodiles') to clear the undergrowth, flush out wildlife and encourage the regrowth of popular food plants throughout Australia is thought to have contributed to reducing the diversity of fire-sensitive plants that populated different landscapes prior to their arrival. Equally likely, however, is that the climatic extremes of wind and drought and resultant fires of the last glacial stage 20,000–18,000 years ago proved to be the final straw for many of the more fire-sensitive species. In south-west Western Australia, excessive fires in parts of the ancient karri forests left only coastal sand dunes in their wake, while in south-eastern Australia, repeated fire changed a landscape with a large component of she-oaks to one dominated by eucalypts. Ironically, the prevalence of open, fire-prone country in many agricultural and pastoral districts today may be a direct result of the reduced plant diversity brought about by periods of high fire frequency.

Eucalypts (*Eucalyptus*, *Corymbia* and *Angophora* spp.) are extremely adaptable plants that can grow in a variety of shapes and sizes from tall shrubs to stunted, multi-stemmed mallees and medium to very tall trees. One characteristic that distinguishes groups of eucalypts is their bark. It can be persistent and rough as in ironbark and bloodwood species, or smooth and matt or shiny and shed either wholly or in part each year as in gum and some apple (*Angophora*) species. Further distinguishing features between similar eucalypts species can be small differences in the shape of the buds, flowers or seed pods, and often species can only be identified during seasons when those features are present. The foliage of some eucalypts changes with age, starting with a rounded leaf shape in the juvenile plant and becoming more elongated as the tree matures.

The average height of eucalypt trees contributes to the classification of forest types — woodlands species grow up to 25 m (82 ft), while those in forest can reach over 50 m (164 ft). The tallest eucalypt species, the mountain ash, can grow up to 100 m (328 ft) tall and unlogged remnants of majestic, perfectly straight-trunked mountain ash forests are found in Victoria and Tasmania. Most eucalypt woodlands and forests are contained within a coastal band extending to around 150 to 600 km (93–375 miles) inland that begins south of the Tropic of Capricorn in Queensland and stretches through New South Wales, Victoria and into South Australia, and can also be found in the south-west pocket of Western Australia.

Across eastern and south-eastern Australia, continuous forests and woodlands once covered much of the country from Queensland's subtropics to the temperate and dry sclerophyll forests that extend through New South Wales into Victoria and South Australia. The fertile land that supported those forests made it highly attractive for agriculture and over 80 per cent of temperate eucalypt forests and woodlands have been cleared since European settlement. The stands of forest and woodlands that remain span landscapes ranging from sparsely covered, drought-prone inland regions to lush mountainous wilderness areas and temperate rainforests.

In the inland regions of south-eastern Australia, a life among dry sclerophyll scrub calls for some ingenious adaptations. West of the Great Divide, rainfall diminishes with increased distance from the coast and is reduced to as little as 180 ml (7 in) per year in the north-west corner of New South Wales. However, such comparative liquid abundance became a longed-for memory when the rains failed to arrive in 2002. For four years, the almost complete absence of rain left the land ravaged as a relentlessly cloudless sky surveyed the fading landscape; over two-thirds of Queensland and almost four-fifths (77 per cent) of New South Wales were officially drought-declared. Dying grasses left expanses of bleached blades in exhausted soils as eucalypts became fully reliant on their famed hardiness. Herds of cattle and sheep perished alongside drying waterholes, and grey kangaroos clustered into desperate, thirsty mobs that invaded farmlands in search of feed and water. Tough though such times are for all who depend on the rains, drought is a part of Australia that has challenged its fauna and flora for millennia and some of the coping mechanisms they have evolved to withstand it are truly remarkable.

Much of the habitat of flying foxes has been cleared since European settlement and large flying fox camps are now often confined to small patches of forest. In permanent camps, trees may consequently become damaged and denuded from overuse by roosting bats.

Wild Australia

The High Country of Victoria and New South Wales comprises Australia's alpine regions and its highest peak, Mount Kosciuszko, reaches only the relatively modest altitude of 2228 m (7300 ft). The vegetation consists largely of heathlands, alpine herbfields and grasslands. Also found here are eucalypts, such as alpine ash and snow gums, that are well adapted to the alpine conditions.

Koala Country: eucalypt forests of the south-east

rising to the challenge

Imagine the following challenge: during a workshop on evolution you are given the following instructions: 'You are to design a mammal that can a. adapt to both arid and temperate conditions, b. live among vast and sprawling landscapes, and c. cope with heat and drought. You may furnish it with a combination of specific physiological and behavioural features to ensure its survival.' Looking at a kangaroo, it is easy to envisage that just such a set of instructions would have brought about this quintessentially Australian design. Kangaroos and their relatives are a diverse group of marsupials that consist of two taxonomic families: the potoroos, bettongs and rat-kangaroos, and the actual kangaroos and wallabies that include the hare-wallabies, nail-tail wallabies, rock wallabies, 'typical' kangaroos and wallabies, and tree-kangaroos.

From their earliest ancestry — kangaroos go back 10 million years while potoroos originated as long as 20 million years ago — this group has been a spectacular success, best illustrated by the kangaroos. Grazers by nature, kangaroos forage on grasses and herbs, and may include leaves, fungi and bark in their diet where these dominate in moister forests. Physically, kangaroos are lean and muscular animals whose large legs and feet (hence 'macropods' or 'big feet', the term often used to describe these animals) are so well constructed that bounding over distances requires a surprisingly small amount of energy. A speedy escape also comes in handy when avoiding predators such as dingoes or fleeing wildfire. A solidly muscular tail helps to balance the animal when standing and acts as a rudder while in motion.

To avoid excessive activity during the heat of the day, kangaroos may forage at night but their peak activity times are during the early morning and early evening. Days are spent resting in the shade of trees or bushes. The kangaroos' most brilliant design feature is a reproductive system that allows them to give birth and raise young when conditions are favourable. During times of drought and little food, hormones allow the female kangaroo to suspend her oestrus cycle and not mate. When food is abundant again and stress is low, the female resumes oestrus, mates, gives birth, and mates again. While the first embryo develops into a joey, the second embryo remains at the post-fertilisation blastocyst stage until the first joey has left the female's pouch. Depending on the external conditions, the activation of the blastocyst may happen relatively quickly or be delayed by up to two years. Some species of kangaroo may have three young at different stages of development at once — one tiny young permanently attached to a teat, an older young-at-foot and intermittently suckling at the second teat, and an undeveloped blastocyst. Kangaroos have well-developed social structures and many live in mobs of several males, females and their offspring.

Young are cared for over many months, ensuring they are well-developed and socialised before becoming independent at around one to one and a half years of age depending on the species. Around Australia, macropods are ubiquitous. While the western woodlands are home to species such as western and eastern greys and wallaroos (euros), habitats of others types of macropods include rainforest, wet and dry eucalypt forest, rocky outcrops and hillsides, mulga and mallee scrub, shrubland, grassland and open desert plains.

forest flagships

Between Queensland and South Australia, the distribution of eucalypts accords with their specific soil, moisture and climate requirements; some occupy very small and specific ranges — one species is only found in the clefts of granite outcrops on mountain tops in a particular region on the Queensland/New South Wales border — while others are widespread and found throughout different landscapes. The majority of wildlife in south-eastern Australia interacts with eucalypt trees at some stage of its life, but the unchallenged king of this terrain is the koala. Koalas were once widespread throughout the forests and woodlands of eastern Australia from Queensland's tropical far north to south-eastern South Australia's drier and cooler climates. Land clearing has restricted this distribution and isolated the South Australian and Victorian populations from those of the east coast. The fundamental dependence of koalas on healthy, continuous forests means that they act as flagships for the forest systems they inhabit; the conservation status of koala populations — sound in some areas, threatened in others — directly reflects the size and health of the forest habitats they rely on.

Koalas occupy a very particular spot in the forest ecosystem. Unlike tree-dwelling possums, gliders, flying foxes and birds that forage on nutrient-rich fruits, flowers or seeds, koalas specialise in feeding on the tough leaves of eucalypts. Eucalypt leaves are low in nutrients and high in toxic chemicals, giving them their distinctively Australian scent but making them a marginal diet at best. To compensate for this, koalas are true connoisseurs of eucalypts and select only the best-quality foliage wherever a choice exists. The nutritional value of the foliage is subject to soil moisture content and fertility, slope and aspect of the tree, and the chemical content of the leaves. Koalas are fussy not only about what types of eucalypts they eat (there are local preferences and seasonal variations), but also about which individual trees they prefer and which leaves on any given tree constitute suitable browse. While foraging, leaves are carefully selected and thoroughly chewed one at a time. Chewing releases starch, sugars and proteins and is the first stage of a long and complex process that requires one of the largest digestive tracts of any

This female eastern grey kangaroo is enjoying a meal of fallen banksia flowers, manipulating them in its front paws. The sweet flowers make a nice change from the grasses and forbs that make up much of its diet.

Koala Country: eucalypt forests of the south-east

Kangaroo joeys enjoy a long period of maternal care. Once it emerges permanently from its mother's pouch, a joey remains with its mother and her mob as 'young-at-heel' and only reaches sexual maturity between one and a half to two years of age.

Young male eastern grey kangaroos mock-wrestle to practice the combat skills they will soon use to defend their females and offspring. The strong, muscular tail serves as a balance, while the broad claws on the hind-feet are aimed towards the opponent's stomach and can cause fatal injury.

Koala Country: eucalypt forests of the south-east

herbivore. The difficult task of processing eucalypt leaves is aided by huge numbers of microbes including bacteria and fungi that ferment the leaves and enable koalas to extract the maximum amount of nutrients while detoxifying and excreting the toxic compounds. There is little waste; once any remaining water has been absorbed towards the end of the digestive process, only a few small, dry fecal pellets are left to excrete, and the efficiency of this process enables koalas to survive long periods of time without drinking.

As flagships for the health of eucalypt forests, the fate of koalas represents that of other wildlife dependent on native forests for its continued survival. Although they were once hunted for food by Aboriginal people and later for their skins by European settlers, the clearing of coastal koala habitat for urban development, agriculture and forestry has had the most significant impact on this species in recent history. The fragmentation of once continuous expanses of forest into separate patches has left many populations isolated and vulnerable to the threats of disease, fire and road traffic. A further consequence of isolation is that koala numbers may increase locally to the point where overbrowsing of eucalypts kills the trees they depend on, leaving the animals to die of starvation. This has occurred on a number of islands (including French, Phillip and Kangaroo Islands) off the South Australian coasts to which koalas were introduced in the early 1900s to counteract local extinctions on the mainland. Like many forest animals, the future of koalas is critically dependent on the protection and sustainable management of native forests.

The clearing and subsequent fragmentation of forests and other natural habitats are common conservation issues not just in Australia but all over the world. Over time, isolation affects the genetics of plants and animals; where migration is impossible, individuals are confined to a remnant patch where they may or may not be able to breed, new bloodlines are cut off, and the regeneration of plants through seed dispersal and pollination is limited. The ability to fly is a strategy that allows many birds and bats to overcome this challenge to a degree, and their importance in the ecological scheme of things has increased considerably as a consequence. A group of flying mammals that shares the koalas' status as forest flagships are the flying foxes. Flying foxes are nocturnal fruit and nectar feeders that are able to make the most of what the seasonal forest menu has to offer — the rainforest fruits of figs, lillipillis and palms, and the nectar of eucalypts, silky oaks, paperbarks and tall flowering shrubs. Owing to their size (a body weight of 0.5 to 1 kg (1.1–2.2 lb) and a wingspan of up to 100 cm (39 in) and high energy needs, flying foxes consume substantial amounts of food in any one night. Travelling distances of up to 60 km (37½ miles) per night depending on the species to food sources uniquely allows them to disperse pollen and seeds between distant forest patches. This is particularly critical for plants that produce most nectar at night and are therefore pollinated at night. Other, smaller nectar-feeders either don't travel the distance or only forage during the day, while smaller fruit-eaters are simply unable to carry the seeds of larger fruit.

Although flying foxes are bats, they have little in common with their smaller, insectivorous microbat cousins. Excellent eyesight and a sharp sense of smell are essential for finding fruit and nectar; the insect-consuming microbats have neither and instead use radar to negotiate the landscape. The two groups owe their differences to a different ancestry — while microbats evolved from a tree-dwelling insect eater, flying foxes are thought to be related to early lemurs. Flying foxes are highly social animals that roost in busy forest canopy camps during the day. A camp may house from several hundred to hundreds of thousands of animals, and individuals recognise each other by their musty scent. As each bat returns to its particular roosting spot at dawn, a quick sniff of the nearest neighbours ensures that all is as it should be. Similar to the impact that koala populations have had on isolated eucalypt patches, the shrinking of native forests has inadvertently increased the impact of flying foxes on confined roosting sites. To enable trees to recover from the damage caused by the roosting bats, camps once shifted through the forest over time. Where such movements are no longer possible and camps are confined to small remnants, damage from overuse can be substantial and the bats are often blamed for defoliation and broken branches while forced to suffer exposure to the elements among a denuded canopy.

birds of the koala country

Along much of the Great Divide, a mild climate and an abundance of flowering and fruiting plants have created a suite of habitats from subtropical and temperate forests to woodlands, coastal heath and sprawling grasslands. Especially in coastal areas, these environments are as much of a home to wildlife as they are to the humans that have settled there. Birds particularly make use of everything these landscapes have to offer. From the larger seeds eaten by cockatoos such as gang gangs, sulphur-crested cockatoos and corellas to the nectar and soft fruit combination preferred by lorikeets and rosellas, the reptiles and invertebrates on the menu of kookaburras, other kingfishers and magpies and the insects gleaned by the small fairy-wrens, pardalotes, treecreepers, bellbirds and robins, the temperate conditions can provide a bounteous yield for the dietary needs of the bird community. At face value, the needs of these birds appear simple and easily met, but many are extremely particular when it comes to aspects such as nesting and breeding. Australia is home to a number of brightly coloured kingfishers that forage in habitats ranging from coastal mangroves to rainforests, woodlands and plains and along rivers, creeks and tidal channels. While this range of habitats suggests considerable variation and adaptability, almost all share an interesting liking for nesting in arboreal termite mounds. As these are porous but large and bulky structures, nest building requires the birds to fly at the mounds with considerable speed and use their long bills to chisel a tunnel into which to lay their eggs. Termite mounds may also be used by the larger kookaburras that are famous for gathering in small groups and announcing their presence with their distinctive laughter-like calls. A close relative of kingfishers, the beautiful and delicately coloured rainbow bee-eater that visits the south-eastern reaches in the summer does not use termite mounds but rather its finely curved beak excavates tunnels into sand banks for nesting.

Among the birds that require trees to nest in, the importance of mature forest and woodland is clearly apparent in the breeding needs of cockatoos, lorikeets and other parrots. All seek out large hollows high up in the trunks of trees as nesting chambers and are therefore dependent on tall and old trees. Hollows happen with age and can be hard to come by as the processes that create them are unpredictable and occur over long periods of time. Fire, lightning strike and the death of a large branch on a mature trunk can initiate a hollow that may take decades to fully form. The value of these old forest survivors is immense; many have been logged or lost, and those that are left are in increasing demand. Competition for prime nesting hollows means that spring in the south-eastern woodlands can be a noisy affair as birds, possums and gliders argue about the best seasonal real estate. Hollows are also sought after by some insectivorous bats and by swarms of introduced bees which have become serious competitors for native wildlife. Often, it's first in, best dressed, but screeching arguments are common as sulphur-crested cockatoos, pink and grey galahs and rainbow lorikeets clash at the premium spots preferred by all. Evictions are not unusual, and a hollow carefully spring-cleaned of old debris by a pair of lorikeets may find itself smugly occupied by an aggressive and much larger cockatoo. The older the tree, the greater its value, and a multi-hollowed giant gum dead or alive can be a hive of activity until the last furred or feathered hatchling has fledged and peace returns.

a sublime soundscape

To the casual observer, the temperate eucalypt woodlands of eastern and southern Australia are perhaps not the most spectacular forest landscapes. Unlike the denser sclerophyll or temperate rainforests that usually offer a diversity of understorey plants (ferns, tree ferns and shrubs or vines), eucalypt woodlands are defined by the sparsity of groundcover. These moderately open landscapes on flat or gently sloping ground have often been converted to farming country, and an appreciation of their more subtle biodiversity that includes beautiful skinks, legless lizards, snakes and beetles among native flowers such as delicate orchids, has often been lost. But despite their more subtle appeal, the south-eastern woodlands offer an experience of great beauty that is often only subliminally associated with this landscape. It is an experience of pure sound, and the first light of day serves as its trigger. Out of the pre-dawn silence, a song of almost spiritual clarity begins and meanders through deep rolling warbles, sliding peaks and moderately pitched crescendos, and dances along a tonal scale in a conversational monologue that may continue for many minutes. In its range and complexity, the song of the magpie is one of the most beautiful of any Australian sounds, as familiar as it is comforting and reassuring. Dawn is not the same without the song of the magpie, and its call is so embedded in the Australian subconscious that it becomes more notable in its absence than its presence.

The soundscape of the south-eastern eucalypt woodlands and forests comprises a suite of fantastic calls made by a range of smallish birds that are usually well concealed. Typically heard in inland woodlands, the tinkling-bounce of a crested bellbird call for one is so amazingly clear that it is difficult to fathom that it could originate from a set of avian vocal chords rather than from a tiny crystal glass being tapped by a spoon. The urgent, lash-like call of the olive-coloured male eastern whipbird by comparison is a feat of lightning-fast vocal acrobatics that stands in sharp contrasts to the female's short double-barrelled reply reminiscent of two short explosive sneezes. But while both bell and whipbirds are aptly named for their calls, neither can compete with the superb lyrebird for its complexity of song and bizarre range of vocal disguises. The ground-foraging lyrebird has an excellent ear for foreign sounds and is able to mimic many to an unnerving resemblance. Chainsaws are a favourite challenge and confuse unsuspecting bush-walkers certain that logging should not be occurring in a national park.

the edge of a continent

Along the south-eastern and southern coasts of Australia, the eucalypt forests and temperate coastal heathlands give way

One of the smaller species of cockatoo, the grey and red gang gang cockatoos occur in the open forest and woodlands of the south-east corner of Victoria and New South Wales and feed on the seeds of trees such as casuarinas and wattles.

◀◀ This rock bridge at Loch Ard Gorge on the Great Ocean Road, in Victoria's Port Campbell National Park has long been separated from the mainland. Inaccessible to people and feral predators, it now provides a safe haven for nesting and roosting birds.

▲ The Otway Ranges in Victoria contain the most western community of cool temperate rainforest in Australia. This moist rainforest originated in Gondwana and, unlike many drier forest types throughout Australia, has no resistance to fire.

Koala Country: eucalypt forests of the south-east

to a breathtaking coastline bordered by beautiful white sand beaches and a string of national parks. Most, like Booderee, Budawang, Murramarang, Eurobodalla, Wadbilliga and the tongue-twisting Croajingolong National Parks, have names that stem from local Aboriginal heritage and describe local landscape features of Aboriginal significance. South of Sydney, forests and the ocean are rarely far apart (except where land has been cleared), and in some areas wildlife such as eastern grey kangaroos may wander onto the beaches while a number of southern right whales frolic in the distance.

One spectacular stretch of coastline in Victoria is the Great Ocean Road. Overlooking Bass Strait and the Tasman Sea along its eastern section and the Southern Ocean past Cape Otway towards the west, this road faces the coldest waters along the Australian coast. In the east, the road begins at Torquay and runs past steep cliff edges, beautiful beaches and tall headlands along the Otway Ranges to Cape Otway, its southernmost point. The forests of the Otways consist of cool temperate rainforest and fern gullies alongside impressive stands of mountain ash, the tallest of the eucalypts. While much of this forest has been logged, the stunning beauty of this area has given rise to a commitment by the Victorian government to buy back outstanding logging licences in order to protect all remaining forest into the future.

The surging ocean along the south coast has been instrumental in shaping a range of natural features. Rock piles, sheer limestone cliffs, blowholes and natural arches abound, and show the coastline itself to be a work in progress at the hands of the elements. One of the oddest natural sculptures is the cluster of granite boulders appropriately called the Remarkable Rocks. Perched on a smooth grey granite dome on the coast of Kangaroo Island in South Australia, the orange lichen-coated rocks appear to have been deliberately placed and then forgotten by time.

Very occasionally, the relentless wear and tear of wind and water on the coastline is witnessed to be a dynamic process. The Twelve Apostles in the ocean off Port Campbell National Park is a grouping of limestone pillars up to 45 m (147 ft) tall and estimated to be over 20 million years old. The pillars were created as the ocean carved deep caves into the coastal limestone cliffs and gradually eroded the base to form arches that subsequently collapsed and left only a number of isolated pillars. Despite their name, the formation comprised only nine Apostles until 2005, when on a Sunday in July, to the amazement of a number of watching tourists, one of the most distinctive pillars conceded to the ocean and spontaneously crumbled into a rocky pile. No less surprised were two other tourists in 1990 who had walked across the nearby arch known as London Bridge when it collapsed behind them and left them stranded on the pillar to be rescued by helicopter. Undoubtedly, theirs were the last human feet ever to stand on that limestone pillar, now forever isolated from human visitors.

'looking after country'

The image of the human footprint on the planet, bearing the weight of our daily — often uninformed — choices, is set to become the most defining metaphor of our time. In Australia, one of the most diverse countries on earth, the impact of that footprint is being felt with crushing force. Changing climates, degraded land and declining freshwater resources are evidence of a continent crying out for help. Thousands of unique plants and animals are under threat of extinction; too many others are already gone. But is it too late? Today, the quality of information about our impact on the environment is unequalled and the options we have to reduce that impact are unprecedented. As Australians, reducing our personal water consumption will conserve diminishing resources, reducing household chemicals will help the environment (and our health), using public transport and choosing sustainable electricity production (rather than coal-fired) will reduce greenhouse gas emissions and a return to native garden plants will help to reduce weeds and save water. While doing the weekly shopping, being better informed about the significant environmental cost of some foods and fibres that require polluting chemicals and excessive water during production will help to make wiser choices at the supermarket shelves. With the smallest effort, personal choices can tip the scales where governments still stubbornly drag their feet. In keeping with the Aboriginal ethos of 'looking after country', it is possible to live with the land rather than at its ultimate expense. Doing nothing is not an option; it will banish many of the wild and remarkable images of this continent to the pages of history.

▲ Contrary to popular belief, flying foxes have a thorough cleaning regime and are rarely dirty. The rough tongue, ideal for licking up nectar and pollen, also makes a great scrubbing tool with which to clean the soft, leathery wings and other body parts in need of grooming.

▲ Flying foxes are utterly confident hanging by just the claws of one foot. Their ankles have ratchet joints that make hanging effortless and unlock when the bats take off in flight.

Flying foxes hanging in dead trees at dusk. As daylight fades, the bats begin to stretch and stir before leaving the day camp in search of food. Once a reliably fruiting or flowering tree has been found, individuals may return to that site over many nights until the food has been exhausted.

Wild Australia 173

Appearing like a sculptural art installation beneath the waterfall, two tree trunks are relentlessly pounded by the falling water that gives them a silver-blue sheen.

Koala Country: eucalypt forests of the south-east

Twelve Apostles at sunset, Port Campbell National Park. Despite their name, the famous limestone pillars off the Victorian coast now number only eight. A ninth pillar collapsed spontaneously in August 2005, leaving only a small pile of rubble, visible here in the foreground on the left.

▲ Resembling a giant feather-duster, the long-legged emu folds up into a compact package while resting.

◀ Wombats are closely related to koalas. Unlike their tree-dwelling cousins, however, wombats live on the ground and dig burrows featuring several tunnels and chambers. To protect their pouch-young while digging, a wombat's pouch faces towards the rear.

▶ Australia's best known marsupial, the koala, was once common throughout eastern Australia's eucalypt forests and woodlands. Koalas were introduced to Kangaroo Island in the 1920s when the South Australian population neared extinction. Since then, numbers on the island have exploded and led to the defoliation and death of many eucalypts. The health of the eucalypts and of the koalas, who starve when foliage runs out, now depends on careful ongoing management.

Koala Country: eucalypt forests of the south-east

While Australia's east coast has many densely populated cities and towns, stretches of coast protected by national parks give a sense of the wilderness that endured until European arrival almost 220 years ago.

Koala Country: eucalypt forests of the south-east

▶ This 'eared' seal, the Australian sea lion, is the only one endemic to Australia and lives on the coasts of Bass Strait, along the South Australian coast and its islands and in south-west Western Australia. This pup and its mother have a strong maternal bond and may stay together for some time after it is weaned at more than a year old.

▼ Both Australian sea lions and New Zealand fur seals live on Kangaroo Island. Unlike sea lions, fur seals have a dense underfur beneath a sleek outer coat of hair. Males reach maturity at 10 years of age and establish territories that are fiercely defended against other males.

Wild Australia

Australian shores are visited by a myriad of seabirds. This silver gull, common along the entire coastline, is seeing out the day at Wilson's Promonotory in Victoria.

Koala Country: eucalypt forests of the south-east

Hovering flocks of crested terns once alerted fishermen to the presence of shoals of fish. This brilliant white and black-capped tern feeds on small fish near the ocean's surface and, once the prey is spotted, plunges out of the sky to grab it.

Wild Australia

▶ Moss- and lichen-covered granite boulders frame the double stream of Ebor Falls in the New England region of New South Wales. Waterfalls and temperate rainforest are distinctive features of this northern region of the state.

◀ While play-fighting within the safe vicinity of their mob, these two young western grey kangaroos are using their forearms to steady themselves on their opponent before leveraging off their tails in order to kick out at each other. Onlookers sometimes misinterpret this behaviour as a friendly hug.

Koala Country: eucalypt forests of the south-east

◀ The Australian pelican, here in striking breeding colours of a pale yellow chest patch and purplish outlined bill and eyes, is a familiar sight on the coast, in ports and wherever there are fishers from which morsels of fish can be scavenged.

▲ Like many areas along Australia's east coast, Murramarang National Park on the New South Wales south coast has a long Aboriginal history. Among the rich environments of wet eucalypt and spotted gum forests and rainforest gullies are fossils that reveal Aboriginal activity dating back 12,000 years. Murramarang contains the largest unmounded Aboriginal midden on the south coast, and the area is still used by Aboriginal people for fishing, recreational and educational activities today.

▲ The crimson rosella comes in no less than six different colour forms (races) — some mainly orange or yellow rather than crimson — that live predominantly in different sections of the tall eucalypt and moist forest areas of the southern east coast. Each race has a local dialect that distinguishes its call slightly from that of a neighbouring race.

◀ Colourful, abundant and vivacious, rainbow lorikeets are common throughout the coastal and near-coastal areas of eastern Australia and feed on nectar, pollen and fruit. A long, rounded, brush-like tongue helps to access the nectar from the often complex flowerheads of plants such as bottlebrushes, grevilleas, banksias and paperbark trees.

▶ The straight-trunked mountain ash is the tallest eucalypt species in Australia. It has been heavily logged for its timber but impressive stands can still be seen in Victoria and Tasmania.

Koala Country: eucalypt forests of the south-east

As the sunlight slowly dissolves the early morning fog, in Victoria's Dandenong Ranges, tall eucalypts strive towards the sky.

Lit by streams of sunlight during the day, in the evenings this cave below a natural rock bridge is brought to life by the pulsating specks of dozens of tiny glow-worms.

related reading

Brooker, I. and Kleinig, D. 1999. *Eucalyptus – an illustrated guide to identification.* Reed New Holland, Sydney, Australia.
Churchill, S. 1999. *Australian Bats.* Reed Natural History, Sydney, Australia.
Cogger, H.G. 2000. *Reptiles and amphibians of Australia.* Reed Books, Sydney, Australia.
Creagh, C. 1992. 'Looking after the land at Uluru'. ECOS No. 71, Autumn 1992.
Dawson, T.J. 1995. *Kangaroos – Biology of the largest marsupials.* University of New South Wales Press Ltd, Australia.
Flannery, T. 1994. *The Future Eaters.* Reed, Sydney, Australia.
Flannery, T. 2005. *The Weathermakers: the history and future impact of climate change.* The Text Publishing Company, Melbourne, Australia.
Higgins, G. and Hermes, N. 1988. *Australia – the land time forgot.* Child and Associates, Australia.
Martin, R. and Handasyde, K. 1999. *The Koala.* Australian Natural History Series, University of New South Wales Press.
Miles, G. 1995. *Wildlife of Kakadu & the Top End of the Northern Territory.* Barker Souvenirs, Alice Springs, Australia.
O'Byrne, D., Bindloss, J., Draffen, A., Finlay, H., Harding, P., Horton, P., McGaurr, L., Mundell, M., Murray, J., Ross, H., Saxton, P. 2000. *Australia.* Lonely Planet Publications, Melbourne, Australia.
Paltridge, R. and McAlpin, S. 2002. *A guide to rare and threatened animals in Central Australia.* WWF Australia, Sydney.
Simpson, K. and Day, N. 2004. *Field Guide to the Birds of Australia* (7th edition). Viking, Australia.
Stanton, J. 2001. *The Australian Geographic Book of the Red Centre.* Australian Geographic, Sydney.
Strahan, R. (ed). 1995. *Mammals of Australia.* Reed, Sydney, Australia.
White, Mary E. 1998. *The greening of Gondwana.* 3rd edition. Kangaroo Press, Australia.
White, Mary E. 1994. *After the greening: the browning of Australia.* Kangaroo Press, Australia.
Wilson, S. and Swan, G. 2003. *A complete guide to reptiles of Australia.* Reed New Holland, Sydney, Australia.

websites

Aboriginal history: www.aboriginalhistory.org
Australian Government Department of Environment and Heritage: www.deh.gov.au
Cooperative Research Centre for Tropical Savannas Management: savanna.ntu.edu.au
Great Barrier Reef Marine Park Authority: www.gbrmpa.gov.au
Environmental Protection Agency/Queensland Parks and Wildlife Service, Wet Tropics Management Authority: www.epa.qld.gov.au/parks_and_forests/world_heritage_areas/wet_tropics
WWF-Australia: www.wwf.org.au

index

Page numbers in bold indicate a photograph.

Aboriginal Land Rights Act 1976 92
Aborigines 16, 19, 36, 43, 46, 92, 134, 140, 157, 158, 165, 185
acacias 91, 96, **105**, **117** *see also* wattles
adaptation 91
agriculture 9
Aire River 8
Alice Springs 92, 95
Anangu Pitjantjatjara 92, 95
Arnhem Land 63
Arnhem Plateau 12
Arrernte 92
Atherton palm 130
Atherton Tableland 126, 133, 134, **139**, 142
Austrobaileya 129
Ayers Rock 12, 92 *see also* Uluru

Babinda Boulders 134, **142**
bangalow palms 126, **127**
banksias 31, 157, **162**
Bartle Frere 129
Bass Strait 179
bats 69, 165: fruit 70; microbats 165
Beauchamp Falls 8
Bell Gorge **24**
bellbirds 165; crested 166
Bellenden Ker 129
Big Ellery Hole **23**
bilbies **49**, 57
billabong **78**
birds 70
birdsnest fern **134**
bloodwoods 91
Blue Mountains 157
boab **41**, 46, **47**
bony bream 95
bottle tree 140
bottlebrush 137, 140, 157
bowerbird, great **54**
Brigalow Belt 137, 140
brolga **76**
Broome 43
budgerigars 43, **56**, 91
buffalo 74
buffel grass 95
Bungle Bungles 12, **33**, 46
Burke and Wills 102
Burke, James 102
burning, traditional **73**

cabbage palms 140, 151
cane toad **74**
Cape Conran Coastal Park **21**
Cape Naturaliste National Park **58**
Cape Otway 171
Cape Peron **38**
Cape Tribulation 145
Cape Wollamai **13**
Cape York 133
Carnarvon Basin 36, 43

Carnarvon Gorge 140, **150**, 151
Carnarvon Gorge National Park 140
cassia 91
cassowary 130; southern 129, 133, **139**
casuarinas 157, 166
catfish, Hyrtl's 95
cats 74
Chewings Ranges 95
claypans 96
climate 12, 137, 171
climate change 6, 20, 32, 129, 134, 137
Cobourg Peninsula 63
cockatoos 165, 166: Carnaby's 32; gang gang 166, **167**; glossy black 157; Major Mitchell's (or pink) cockatoo **105**; palm 133; red-tailed black 32, 157
colonisation 31
coneflowers 31
controlled burns 68
coolabahs 91, 96
copper laurel 129
coral 134
corellas 43, **79**, **125**
crimson rosella **186**
crocodile **67**, 69, 70, **85**
crow **98–99**, 100
crown-of-thorns starfish 137
cuscus, grey 133; spotted 133
cycads 95, 140, 151

Daintree rainforest 126, 129
daisies 91
Dampier Peninsula 43
Dampier, William 36
Dandenong Ranges **188**
date-palm 101
desert 28, 88, 95, 96
desert oak 91, **104**, **118**
desert rainbowfish 95
Devil's Marbles **123**, **124**
dieback 32
dingo 16, **119**
dolphin, bottlenose 36
dragon, Boyd's forest 130, 152, **153**; eastern water **143**
drought 158, 161
dry season 60, 64
dryandra 31
Drysdale River 43
ducks, wandering whistling **83**
dugongs 36

eagle, wedge-tailed **55**, 69, 95, 100, **125**
Ebor Falls **183**
echidna 140
egret, white **77**
emu 43, **176**
emu bush 91
erosion 9
eucalypts **23**, 31, **48**, 95, 158, 160, 161, 165, 166, 170, **176**, 188
Eungella 140

Eungella National Park 137
euro 69 *see also* wallaroo
evolution 16
Eyre, Edward John 31

fairy-wrens 165
fan palm 130
farming 19
fig trees 140
figs 130
finches 70, 91; Gouldian **56**, 70
Finke Gorge National Park 95
Finke River 95, 102, 114
fire 12, 15, 19, 58, **73**, 91, 158, 166
fire-stick farming 19
flood 64
flying foxes 32, 70, 157, **159**, 165, **172**, **173**: spectacled 133
François Peron National Park **57**
frogs 137: giant (or white-lipped) tree 130; green tree **134**; northern banjo **151**; northern dwarf tree 130; Spencer's burrowing 96, **109**; stony-creek **148**
fruit bat 70
fur seal, New Zealand **179**

Gagadju 63
galah **110**
Gamba grass 74
geckoes 96: knob-tailed **112–113**, **114**; leaf-tailed **131**
geology 12
gibber desert 96, 101
gidgee 91, 96
gliders 140, 157
glow-worms **189**
goannas 69
goby, Finke 96
gold 134
Gondwana 9, 12, 15, 157
grasses 95
Great Artesian Basin 140
Great Barrier Reef **128**, 134, 137
Great Ocean Road **26**, 170, 171
Great Sandy Desert 43
Great Victoria Desert 28
Greater Blue Mountains World Heritage Area 154
grevilleas 31, 91, 157
guava, native 129
gull, silver **180**
gum trees: ghost 91, 95; red 31; river red 91; Sydney blue 137 *see also* eucalypts
Gwion Gwion paintings 43

hakeas 91, 157
Hamersley Range 43 *see also* Karijini National Park
Hancock Gorge **45**
hardyhead, Finke 95
Hartog, Dirk 36
hawk, crested 69
Heavitree Ranges 95
heron, pied **82**

hibiscus 91
hibiscus, native 140
Homo sapiens 91
honey myrtle 157
honeyeaters 70, 157: Eungella 137

introduced species 74, 102, 166
iron ore 43
ironwood 95

jacana, comb-crested **66**
jarrah 31, 32
Jaru people 46
Jawoyn people 63
Jim Jim Creek **62**

Kakadu 63
Kakadu National Park 60, **62**
Kalbarri National Park **44**, **59**
Kangaroo Island **156**, 171, **179**
kangaroo paws 31
kangaroos 96, 161, **163**: eastern grey **27**, 161, **162**, **164**; red 101; western grey 161, **182**, 183
Karijini National Park **34–35**, 36, 39, **45**, 49
karri **30**, 31
Kata Tjuta 12, 92, 95, 100, **121**
Kija people 46
Kimberley 4, 12, 24, 28, 32, 43, 46
king fern 130
King, Governor Philip 157
kingfisher 165, 166
kites 69: black 46
koala 32, 161, 165, **176**, **177**
kookaburras 165, 166: blue-winged **87**
Kuku Yalanji 134
kultarr 96

Lake Eacham rainbow fish 129
Lake Eyre 96
Lake Eyre Basin 96
law, traditional 92
Leeuwin-Naturaliste National Park 51
Leichhardt, Ludwig 63
licuala 130
Litchfield National Park 72, 74, **75**
Livistona palms 140
lizards: frilled 60, **61**, 69; shingle-back 101
Loch Ard Gorge **168–169**, 170
London Bridge **26**
lorikeets 157, 165, 166: red-collared 70, **71**
lotus lily **66**
lowland forests 69
lyrebird, superb 166

MacDonnell Ranges 95, **103**
Mackay tulip oak 137
macropods 69, 161
magpie 165
mallee 91, 161
malleefowl 57

mammals 15, 16, 133, 140, 161
mangrove palms 130
mangroves **145**
Marble Bar 28
marri 31, 32
marsupials 16, 161
Mary River **79**
megafauna 19
microbats 165
Millstream-Chichester National Park **18**, 39
Mirrar people 63
mogurnda, Finke 95
mole, marsupial 96
Mon Repos **136**
monitors 69, 96: lace 140; Merten's water **72**; yellow spotted **49**
Monkey Mia 36
monotremes 16, 140
monsoon 81
monsoon forest 69
Mount Kosciuszko **160**
Mount Olga 92
mountain ash 158, 186, **187**
mouse: dusky hopping 96; spinifex hopping 96
mulga 91, 95, 96, 161
mulla mulla **22**, 91
Mungo National Park **6, 7**
Murramarang National Park **185**
Myrtaceae 31, 157
mythology 123, 134

Nambung National Park 36, **52**
Napier Range 46
natural gas 43
natural springs 101
New Guinea 133
Ningaloo Marine Park 39
Nullabor Plain 12, 28
numbat 32

Oenpelli 63
oil 43
Olgas, The 12
orchids 140
Ormiston Gorge **103, 114**
Otway Ranges **8, 170, 171**
owls 140: barking 69, **81**

Palm Valley 95
paperbark trees **62, 68, 84,** 91, 101, 157
Papilionaceae 31

parakeelya 91, **106**
pardalotes 165
parrots: eclectus 133, **138, 139**; ringneck **94**
pea flowers 91
pearling 43
pelican, Australian **184,** 185
Pentecost River **37**
pepper tree 129
perentie **115, 116**
pharmaceuticals 129
Phillip Island **13**
piccabeen 126, **127**
pigeon, spinifex **122**
Pilbara 18, 28, 36, 39, 43, **48**
Pilbara Ranges 39
Pinnacles Desert 36
pioneers 63
Pitjantjatjara 92
platypus 140, **151**
playas 96, 97
pollution 137
Port Campbell National Park **26,** 170, 171, **175**
possums 140, 157: green **134**; Herbert River ringtail **134**; striped 133
potoroo, Gilbert's 32
Proteaceae 31, 157
Purnululu **33,** 46
Purnululu National Park 28, **29, 33**

quandong, blue 130
Queensland 126
quoll, northern 69

rainbow bee-eater 166
rainbow lorikeets **186**
rainbow pittas 69
Rainbow Valley **108**
rainfall 28
rat-kangaroo, musky 130
Red Bluff **44**
red cabbage palm 95
Redbank Gorge **88, 89**
Remarkable Rocks **156,** 171
river she-oaks 137
robins 165
rock art 43, 140
Roebuck Bay 43, 46
rose-crowned fruit dove 69
rosellas 165

sacred sites 92

saltbush 95, 101
saltlake 96, **97**
saltpans 97
sandhill canegrass 96
savannas 95
scarlet-sided pobblebonk **151**
sclerophyll scrub 157, 158
scrubfowl, orange-footed 69
sea levels 12, 15
sea lion, Australian **179**
settlers 165
Shark Bay 12, 32, 39
Shark Bay World Heritage Area 36, 57
Shell Beach 36
she-oaks 157
Simpson Desert **10,** 96, 102, **107, 111**
skinks 96: blue-tongue **90**; orange-sided 137
snakes 96: amethyst python **25, 152**; green tree 134, **135, 149**; python **64, 65**; scrub python **25**; tree 130, **149**
songlines 19
spider flowers 157
spinifex grass **18,** 91, 95, **118**
stinging tree 130
stromatolites 39
Stuart Creek 102
Stuart Highway 101
Stuart, John McDouall 63, 102
Sturt's desert pea **106**
Sturt's Stony Desert **10, 11,** 101
sugarcane 129
Sugarloaf Rock **51**
swan, black **132**
Sydney Basin 154

Tanami desert 102
Tarra Bulge National Park 16, **17**
Tasmanian devil 16
Tasmanian tiger 16
tea trees 157
Tennant Creek 102
termite mounds 166
termites 32
tern, crested **181**
thorny devil **10, 53,** 101
tjukurpa 92
Tolmer Falls **74, 75**
Torquay 171
tortoise, western swamp 32
tree ferns 130

treecreepers 165
tree-kangaroos 133: Bennett's 133; Lumholtz tree-kangaroo 129, 133, 134, **147**
tropical rainforest 126, 129
tropicbird, red-tailed **51**
trout, ocean 46
turtles: freshwater **50**; loggerhead **136**
Twelve Apostles 171, **175**

Uluru 12, 92, **93** see also Ayers Rock
Uluru-Kata Tjuta National Park **14,** 118
uranium 63

volcanic activity 12

waddy-wood 96
wallabies **140**: agile 140, **141**; red-necked 154, **155**; rock 95
wallaroos **40,** 69, 161: black 69 see also euro
Walls of China **6, 7**
Wandjina paintings 46
wandoo 32
waratahs 157
Warren National Park **30**
wasps, fig 130
waterbirds 64
wattles 91, **117, 118, 121,** 166
West MacDonnell Ranges **23,** 88
wet season 60, 64, 84, **85, 86**
Wet Tropics 130, 133, 134, 137
Wet Tropics World Heritage Area 129
whale shark 39
whale, humpback 36
whipbird, eastern 166
wildfires 15, 56, 68, 73, 91, 158
wildflowers 31
Wills, John 102
Wilson's Promontory **180**
Windjana Gorge **22,** 46
Wollemi pine 157
wombat **176**
wompoo fruit-dove 130
Wooramel seagrass bank 36
woylies 57

Yalariji 134
Yawuru people 43
Yellow Water lagoon 83